In all my years of exploring the powe
that the true expression of leadership is fou_
the incredible story of Dino Rizzo and Healing Place Church and have
seen the eternal impact that serving has made on so many lives in their
community and throughout the world. *Servolution* is a must-read for anyone who wants to transform their life and the lives of others simply by
choosing to serve with no strings attached.

—John C. Maxwell
Author, Speaker, and Founder of EQUIP

Dino Rizzo is one of those guys you can't not like. His love for God and
for people is contagious. And his book, *Servolution*, is a must-read. It is inspi-
rational. It is practical. And it has the potential to revolutionize your life.

—Mark Batterson
Lead Pastor, National Community Church

In *Servolution*, Dino Rizzo has done a fabulous job of revealing God's
heart for a hurting world and what each one of us can do to bring healing
to those around us. In this book, we get not only a wealth of information but also real stories of someone who lives out what he teaches. Dino
inspires me like few others I know.

—Chris Hodges
Senior Pastor, Church of the Highlands

Dino Rizzo attracts miracles! Why? Because he serves people everywhere he goes. I know from serving people on the streets of New York
City that miracles follow serving. This book is the story of miracles that
have come to Dino and Healing Place Church because of their commitment to serving others with no strings attached. Read, study, and implement what the Spirit says to you through this book and get ready to see
miracles in your church.

—Nelson Searcy
Lead Pastor, The Journey Church

I have never known anyone who lives and breathes the concept of
"servolution" as much as Dino Rizzo does. This tool is a huge win for the
church. For years we have asked Dino to take the time to break down

this concept and write out practical steps so that everyone can tap into it. Let's go for it!

—Rick Bezet
New Life Church

Matthew 11:12: "Since the days of John the Baptist, the Kingdom of God has been forcefully advancing and forceful men lay hold of it." Dino Rizzo is a dynamo helping to advance the kingdom of God. His heart for the poor, oppressed, and the needy is precious. This book will stimulate your resolve to serve and advance the kingdom.

—Bill McCartney
CEO, Promise Keepers

Dino Rizzo oozes servolution from his pores, which is both inspiring and contagious. Once you join this revolution, there's no looking back. Serving the poor is one of the most powerful ways to demonstrate Christ's love, and Dino does an amazing job showing us the way. This book will change the world.

—Anne Jackson
Author, *Mad Church Disease*

Dino Rizzo's life, passion, and enthusiasm more than qualify him to speak with influence on the topic of servanthood. Healing Place Church is a great example of a church filled with kingdom-driven, servant-minded, community focused people, and they are strategically bringing change to the nation. This book is about team, it's about vision, and it will inspire you to a fresh and radical way of living.

—Brian Houston
Senior Pastor, Hillsong Church

Dino Rizzo has masterfully captured this much-needed message not only with the words he has written but also with the life he has lived. This book is for every pastor, every church, and every believer who wants to fulfill God's mandate on this earth. Don't just read this book with your eyes; let its message sink into the depths of your soul.

—Priscilla Shirer
Author and Bible Teacher

SERVOLUTION

The Leadership Network Innovation Series

The Big Idea: Focus the Message, Multiply the Impact, Dave Ferguson, Jon Ferguson, and Eric Bramlett

Confessions of a Reformission Rev.: Hard Lessons from an Emerging Missional Church, Mark Driscoll

Deliberate Simplicity: How the Church Does More by Doing Less, Dave Browning

Leadership from the Inside Out: Examining the Inner Life of a Healthy Church Leader, Kevin Harney

The Monkey and the Fish: Liquid Leadership for a Third-Culture Church, Dave Gibbons

The Multi-Site Church Revolution: Being One Church in Many Locations, Geoff Surratt, Greg Ligon, and Warren Bird

Sticky Church, Larry Osborne

SERVOLUTION

STARTING A CHURCH REVOLUTION THROUGH SERVING

DINO RIZZO

FOREWORD BY CRAIG GROESHEL

 ZONDERVAN®

ZONDERVAN.com/
AUTHORTRACKER
follow your favorite authors

We want to hear from you. Please send your comments about this book to us in care of zreview@zondervan.com. Thank you.

ZONDERVAN

Servolution
Copyright © 2009 by Dino Rizzo

Requests for information should be addressed to:

Zondervan, *Grand Rapids, Michigan* 49530

Library of Congress Cataloging-in-Publication Data

Rizzo, Dino, 1964 –
    Servolution : starting a church revolution through serving / Dino Rizzo.
    p. cm.
    Includes bibliographical references.
    ISBN 978-0-310-28763-6 (softcover)
    1. Evangelistic work. 2. Service (Theology) 3. Healing Place Church. I. Title.
    BV3793.R58 2009
    253 – dc22   2008049749

Interior design by Matthew Van Zomeren

Printed in the United States of America

09 10 11 12 13 14 15 • 20 19 18 17 16 15 14 13 12 1 10 9 8 7 6 5 4 3 2 1

This book is dedicated first and foremost
to my Lord and Savior, Jesus Christ,
who is the greatest servant of all

Also to my wife, DeLynn, the love of my life

And to my incredible, beautiful children,
McCall, Dylan, and Isabella

In loving memory of my father and mother,
Robert and Gloria Rizzo,

and to my father- and mother-in-law,
Wayne and Dee Austin

To the people of Healing Place Church

And to every pastor who has stayed up late
and gotten up early to serve and to care for
the people Jesus died for

CONTENTS

FOREWORD

Some leaders push me. Some inspire me. Some challenge me. But Dino Rizzo is a leader who messed me up — in the best sort of way. And that's what he is about to do to you.

For several years I'd heard about this radically generous, utterly selfless, kingdom-minded Cajun from the deep woods of Louisiana. Most LSU fans are a bit different anyway. (Sorry Tigers.) But Dino is off-the-charts different!

My first extended time with Dino and his Healing Place Church family was when I was in Baton Rouge touring the church's campuses. Within moments of our plane's landing, Dino proudly showed us around his Dream Center campus. His eyes clearly revealed his heart. One moment, they bounced with passion as he explained how the people of his church were making a difference helping those who had much less than they did. The next moment, his eyes filled with tears as he described in detail the single mom with three children who had been abused for years. Every person we met, Dino hugged, high-fived, and bragged on. I've rarely seen more love from a pastor for his people.

Our next stop was a tour of the medical mobile units. I met a doctor who treats people for no charge on the weekends, a dentist who had just pulled forty-one teeth that needed to come out, and dozens of other people who were along for the ride — simply to show the love of Christ. We met leaders from the city. Firefighters. Police officers. City council members. All who had become a part of this great church after they had been served by the church.

These people are *different*. They are obsessed with serving without expecting anything in return. It isn't something they think about doing. It is who they are. They are not just church attenders. They are servants on a mission to impact their city with the love of Christ.

It rattled me. We were making a difference in the lives of people *inside* our church. These people were making a difference in the lives of people outside their church. They were living the life I'd read about in the book of Acts. And they were seeing similar miraculous New Testament results.

This is the way it is supposed to be. This is the kingdom of God.

If you're looking for a book with church-growth techniques, clever ideas, or the latest theories, put this one down. Instead of programs, tactics, and strategies, you'll experience stories that will move you, compel you, and disturb you out of your comfort zone into a life of radical kingdom servanthood. I'm confident Dino's story will mess you up—in the best sort of way. In your life and ministry, let the servolution begin!

—Craig Groeschel, Senior Pastor, LifeChurch.tv

ACKNOWLEDGMENTS

I want to extend my sincere thanks and deep appreciation to those who have shared this *Servolution* journey with me:

Greg Ligon, Mark Sweeney, and the Leadership Network team: Thanks for the privilege of being allowed to be a part of the Innovation Series.

Paul Engle, Mike Cook, Chris Fann, Ryan Pazdur, Brian Phipps, and the team at Zondervan: Thanks for your partnership in the kingdom and thank you for believing in us.

Dan and Vicki Ohlerking, Molly Venske, and Lance LeBlanc: You are the greatest! I appreciate all your hard work and diligence in this project. Without your encouragement and excellence, this would not have been possible.

Earl Rentz: You are "the real deal" who has believed in me from the beginning. You're the best!

Mike Haman: You make me "too blessed to be depressed"! Love you and all your "Hamanisms"!

To the Healing Place Church staff, leaders, and volunteers: You are the greatest church on the planet. It is your heart to serve that has truly ignited our servolution, and it is why I love doing life with you. Your humility, extreme generosity, and compassion for the poor and hurting take my breath away. Your passion to serve has inspired me, as it has many others around the world, and I believe our greatest opportunities lie ahead.

And thanks to DeLynn: Thanks for always believing in me. Together we can accomplish more than we could ever dream. I will love you forever.

WE CAN'T LET THIS ONE GET AWAY

I showed my dad her picture. I was twenty-two, had met the girl of my dreams, and somehow I had gotten her to agree to marry me. My dad looked at the picture, then he looked at me, then the picture, then me. It wasn't adding up. After a few moments of silence, he finally concluded this must be an act of Almighty God. It could only be a blessing from a merciful God that such a beautiful girl would soon be his daughter-in-law.

I had asked DeLynn to marry me, but since I didn't have the funds for the ring yet, I had come home to talk to my dad, picture in hand as proof of the miracle. He turned to me, bowed up his chest, and told me, "Son, we've got to get a ring on her finger right away. We can't let this one get away."

He walked into the other room and came back with an envelope and handed it to me. To my surprise, it was loaded with cash he had set aside for me months earlier. I knew my full-blooded Italian father was about to make me an offer I could not refuse. He smiled at me and said, "Let's buy the biggest diamond we can find and get it on this gorgeous girl's finger." So we did.

Now, more than twenty years later, every time I look at DeLynn's hand and see her ring, I can still hear my dad's voice and the intensity in his eyes as he said to me, "We can't let this one get away."

Just as my father was unwilling to let the blessing of this beautiful daughter-in-law slip away, I believe our heavenly Father feels the same way for the lost. The heart of God Almighty sees the people in our homes, in our cities, in the cubicles next to us, and down the street. He values them as prizes He is unwilling to go without, and He looks intently into our hearts and says, "Let's do whatever it takes—no matter the cost. We can't let them get away!"

Throughout the Bible, God's cry is heard as He calls out to His people to notice others. Others in nursing homes, others without homes, others living without fathers, others living dysfunctional lives, others working in strip clubs or selling their bodies, others next door, and others around the world. Because of His intense love for the world, He sent His son to die for us, and whoever believes in Jesus—*whoever* believes—will be saved. In Jude 23, we are encouraged to help others who are doubting, to snatch others from the fire, to show mercy to others around us.

If we will listen carefully, we will hear our Father telling us, "I love you, I care about you, and I will move heaven and earth for you. But I don't see only you; I see beyond you as well. You belong to Me. And because you're so precious to Me, I want to have you join Me in My mission to reach others." He wants to have us share in His joy of seeing others find hope and healing in Jesus. That's what He was telling us when He said, "I've come to seek and to save what was lost."[1] We cannot let them get away.

Our lives represent more to God than we could ever imagine—so many lives and so many people to be brought to Him. Just like an apple seed holds within it the potential of producing a new tree, which in turn will bear thousands of other apples, so it is with our lives. If we could see what God sees in us and what each of our lives could mean for His kingdom, we would be blown away. There are others who can be reached through us, and in addition, there are others in our others. God is counting on us to rise up and make the difference.

My hope is that through the story of our ongoing journey, Christians will be awakened to see the world from a new perspective, that we will not wake up thinking, "How can I grow my church today?" or "How can I improve my career today?" but rather that the first thought in our hearts every morning will be, "How can I serve the people in my life today? How can I reach out and care for those who live next door and work in the same office with me?"

We may never know until we get to heaven how our service and our simple acts of kindness have affected the course of a life, a community, or even a nation. If we do nothing, the result will be — nothing! However, when we engage in a pursuit to serve others, and a servolution is ignited to care for the hurting around us, we will witness the most amazing results. People will find hope and healing that can be found only in Jesus. We will find that we are part of something much bigger than ourselves as we join with Him in building His kingdom.

I invite you to join a movement that is rumbling throughout the body of Christ, a revolutionary army of people ready to take up this mandate. We are actively pursuing the lost, the forgotten, and the poor to show them a God who is passionately in love with them. We stand ready with one heart, saying, "We are here to do whatever, whenever, so that the others will not get away. We will serve others and show them the hope that can come only from Jesus."

This is a revolution of serving others — a servolution. The troops are followers of Christ, the companies of soldiers are churches, and the weapons are towels for service. Once you have experienced the sense of purpose that comes from serving others with every bit of energy, time, and resources you possess, you'll want to serve more and more. And as you do, you'll be plundering hell and populating heaven. Through our lives, through our families, and through our churches, God is about to touch the lives of others in ways we never dreamed possible.

CHAPTER 1

THE BEGINNING OF A SERVOLUTION

FORTY-FIVE TONS OF TEA

I wonder if they knew they were about to spark a revolution. Did they realize that this one evening of action would ignite the fuse for the American Revolution? Did they have any idea that what they were doing would alter history as they knew it and change the world forever? On December 16, 1773,[1] three hundred Sons of Liberty marched onto several tea ships docked in Boston Harbor. As a protest against unfair taxation, they methodically dumped over forty-five tons of British tea into the water. As thousands of colonists cheered them on, I wonder if they understood the significance of their protest.

The Boston Tea Party is a great example of what it takes for a revolution to begin: a clear mission that everyone believes in, people who will not stand for oppression, and leaders who are willing to lay down their lives to initiate change. We see examples of revolutions all throughout the history of the world and hear the testimonies of the brave heroes who gave their lives for their cause.

This book is about revolution. But this is a different kind of revolution — not one fueled by anger, violence, and revolt but one of compassion, love, and service. This revolution has a clear mission to answer the cries of the poor, the hurting, and the forgotten and is made up of revolutionaries willing to lay down their lives to reach out to people in their cities, in their nations, and throughout the world. This is a revolution aimed at initiating change, but not by overthrowing a government; this change comes by bringing healing to a hurting world and by loving people to Christ.

We call it a servolution: a significant change in the course of history sparked by simple acts of kindness.

What Is a Servolution? (surv-uh-loo'-shuhn)
1. A complete and radical change of a person's life caused by simple acts of kindness for the glory of God.
2. God's kingdom on earth as it is in heaven.
3. A church revolution through serving.

I cannot speak for the Sons of Liberty who jump-started the American Revolution, but when our servolution began, DeLynn and I didn't know what kind of impact it would have or the number of people that would be affected. It didn't have a name, and there certainly weren't thousands of onlookers cheering us on. We were just two young people who had an intense desire in our hearts to demonstrate Christ's love to people and to serve hurting families in our community. We believed if we could lead a church with a heartbeat to reach the world by serving one person at a time, something amazing would happen,[2] but we had no idea just how far God would take us.

The purpose of this book is not to lay out a formula for pastors to grow a church or how a Christian can revolutionize his or her life. There is no easy ten-step program to start your servolution. Everyone's path will be unique. And while we have done many things right at Healing Place Church so far, we also have experienced our share of act-now-and-figure-it-out-later moments. There is no perfect equation for anything God calls us to do, but it's always exciting to pursue our destiny in Him!

SPARKS FLY

One of the initial sparks of this servolution was also one of the most humbling experiences of my life. DeLynn and I had been married just a few years and we were visiting Houston during a major crossroad in our lives. We had recently resigned our position as youth pastors at the church where we met, and had spent several months speaking to churches and youth camps across the country. Although we had been offered quite a few ministry opportunities, we were not settled on exactly where God wanted us to go.

In October of 1993, we found ourselves in the living room of Pastor John Osteen, the founder of Lakewood Church.[3] Pastor Osteen was a legend for many people — including DeLynn and me — and here we were, privileged to visit with him in his home with the family he loved so much. I was asking questions left and right, wanting to learn from this man I respected so much. Then he floored me with a question of his own: "Son, what do you want to do? What has God placed on your heart to do?"

There were so many thoughts and dreams DeLynn and I had been trying to process. At first, I didn't know what to say. We didn't have it all sorted out, but I wanted so badly to be able to explain what we were feeling in our hearts. So when I started to answer him, it all just spilled out. It was one of those moments when you don't even know what you are saying. You're so full of dreams, ideas, and questions you can't hold back, and like a dam bursting, the words keep flowing. Finally, I ran out of words to say, having put it all on the line.

I didn't know how I really expected him to respond. I honestly wasn't too sure what I had just said, but somehow I hoped he would have some great advice to share with me. Instead, Pastor Osteen simply looked at me. The silence was deafening, and I began to replay it all in my head. *Did I say all that out loud?* Suddenly, I had that bad-dream feeling like I was standing in a spotlight at center court during the opening of the NBA finals wearing only my boxers. *Oh, man. I don't even want to imagine what Pastor Osteen is thinking right now.*

Then he stood up and walked out of the room. He just got up and left! So I did what any good husband would do in this situation; I passed the buck to my wife. "DeLynn, why didn't you stop me? Give me 'the look,' kick my shin, pour your drink on me — *anything!*"

Man.

After a three-minute eternity, he came back and surprised me by handing me a check for four hundred dollars. He said, "Here's what you need to do. You need to start a church in Baton Rouge to reach the poor and hurting. Here's the first tithe: I'm giving you your first offering." He had listened to our hearts and had the wisdom to tell us that what DeLynn and I knew deep inside was what God wanted for our lives.

And then, in his own kidding-but-not-really way he told me, "Now if you *don't* start that church, I'm going to come and have you thrown in jail because you stole my money." I took those words very seriously as I carried that yellow four hundred dollar check signed by John Osteen back to Baton Rouge.

And that was that. DeLynn and I drove home to start a church, not because John Osteen told us to but because he had helped us recognize what God had already put in our hearts, and he had helped us muster the courage to step out and do it.

That simple act of handing us a check changed the course of our history. Looking back, it was one of the sparks that ignited our servolution. It was a God-moment for us. We knew our mission. We had our mandate.

We knew we had some enormous challenges ahead, but we were determined to succeed. Baton Rouge was a community with countless hurting people. It was 1993, and the city was still reeling from several high-profile ministry scandals.[4] Many people had given up on church and, even worse, had given up on God. In addition, Louisiana typically ranks as one of the top states in nearly every negative category: poverty, illiteracy, unemployment, and quality of life.

Our first challenge came the first time I spoke at our new church and twelve people showed up. After I preached, five of them quit. I did the math and figured out if my preaching continued to drop our attendance by 42 percent each service, I had only two more weeks until the place would be empty.

I did the math and figured out if my preaching continued to drop our attendance by 42 percent each service, I had only two more weeks until the place would be empty.

Nice.

Needless to say, we were very discouraged, so DeLynn and I decided to drown our sorrows by partaking in each of the thirty-one Baskin Robbins' flavors. Our discouragement didn't last long, though, because somewhere around flavor twenty-seven, we remembered why we had gotten into this in the first place. We knew God had called us to love and help the poor and the hurting, and we resolved that no matter how many people came to (or left) the church, we would not throw in the towel. We were not going to care about the numbers; we would simply do our part to love and serve people, and leave the church growth up to God.

We made a game plan for the week ahead that consisted of one major play: do whatever we can to help the people of our community. It sounds simple enough, but where do you start with something like that? We began to scour the newspapers to find out what was going on in our community. We tried to identify the people no one else was serving or thinking about. What needs were there? Who was being overlooked? Who were others unwilling to serve or just unable to help? As soon as we began looking, it was easy to find people who were ready for a servolution, and we started serving them in any way we could. We contacted organizations that were having big events and asked if we could help them clean up afterward. We found couples who had just become parents and brought them diapers and formula. We visited elderly people who were sick, and cooked meals for the families of people who were hospitalized. And soon one thing began leading to another.

SERVE SOMEBODY

Since the church was new and very small, there wasn't much office work to be done. One day, it was only 10:00 a.m. and both items on the day's to-do list were already completed: I had cut the grass at the church and run the weed eater. Instead of simply sitting there, I decided to get to work serving somebody. I read through some cards that visitors to the church had filled out and learned that one of the ladies was a widow and was dying of cancer.

I went to a grocery store, bought a pack of flowers for seven dollars, and then a couple of us drove to her house so we could visit her. We gave her the flowers and told her we loved her. It wasn't anything elaborate, but this simple act of kindness meant the world to her. We sat and talked for quite a while, and as we were leaving, she said, "I have a few friends who are also widows. Would you visit them too?" So the next week we visited four widows, then ten widows the following week, and the number of widows being visited has continued to grow ever since.[5]

Here's what I discovered. Each one of these ladies had a family with needs, ready to be helped. "Can you call my son? He needs to be in church." "Can you call my daughters? They would love to be a part of a church like this." As we served our way into these widows' lives, their worlds opened up to us, along with more people and more opportunities to demonstrate the love of Jesus. The next thing we knew, there were a hundred people in our church, then two hundred, and the number is still growing. The preaching, the music, and the singing were all the same, but we grew because we were committed to serving the people of our community one by one. Our attitude was "whatever, whenever." I know now that this kind of heart to generously bless others is the perfect catalyst for a servolution. Jesus said it this way: "It is more blessed to give than to receive."[6]

As new people came to the church, new needs and new opportunities to serve came along with them. I was in a prayer meeting one night, and a woman raised her hand and said, "My boyfriend just left me. I need to move out of our apartment tomorrow and I don't have a truck or any help." The leader said, "Well, we'll be in prayer for you." I was sitting in the back of the room thinking, *This woman needs more than a prayer; she also needs a Chevy pickup. How can we get her a truck and some volunteers with strong backs?*

The next day I got a few men together and we showed up at her apartment with a truck ready to help her move. We had everything packed within two hours, and we moved her and her baby to her parents' house before lunchtime. She was so grateful and touched by this simple act that she started attending our services faithfully. And when her family realized a church had taken care of their daughter and granddaughter without asking for anything in return, *they* started to come to church. Then it dawned on me: we could really reach a lot of people this way! Sure enough, word got around and we ended up helping a whole lot of single moms over the next few months.

Another way we began to reach out to people in our community was by performing weddings for people who were not in our church and even for those who were not yet believers. Our thought was that we'll do their weddings as long as they'll agree to come to several hours of premarital counseling, during which we'll make the gospel message very clear. As it turned out, many of the couples ended up giving their lives to Christ during the process, and because of this, we still use this approach today as an outreach to our community. Sure, we receive a little flack for being so "unspiritual as to allow heathens to be married in our church," but we have never regretted it for one moment.

One of the couples we married was an LSU football player named Kevin and a girl named Tracy, whom DeLynn went to high school with. Tracy came from a strong Christian family but was struggling in her walk with Christ, and Kevin wasn't even pretending to be a Christian. But when they asked us to marry them, we did. They sat through the sessions and listened, but they weren't ready to commit their lives to Christ.

After the wedding, we rarely heard from them. Kevin went on to play football in the NFL, and they lived out of town most of the time. Then one day Kevin called and said he needed to talk to me. His brother had been killed in a car accident, and Kevin had several questions about God he wanted to ask me. He said I was the only person he could think of who could help him.

When we met, Kevin began to go through a notebook full of tough, heartfelt questions he had written down. After a few minutes, I stopped him and said, "Kevin, I can't even begin to answer all the questions you have, but I think you've already got a lot of this figured out. It seems like what you're missing is just the willingness to put your faith in God and trust Him with your life." And in a few minutes we were praying together as he surrendered his life to Jesus.

What would have happened if we had told Kevin and Tracy we wouldn't marry them because they were not part of our church or not living for God? There's no way they would have come our way when they were facing a crisis in their lives. But thank God they did. Today, Kevin plays for the Tennessee Titans and is the president of the NFL Players Association. More important, he and Tracy are living out a fantastic testimony of God's grace and mercy.[7]

It seemed like the more ways we served, the more the people in the church began to offer creative ideas for reaching out to our community. One of our ladies mentioned that she thought it would be nice if we had a meal for everyone after the Sunday service. She was envisioning a potluck dinner, for which each family brings a casserole. But you and I both know that far too often people use potluck dinners as opportunities to try out new recipes for spam soup, filet o'squash casserole, or peanut butter and black bean cobbler. And in Louisiana, it can get even scarier: I've seen some crazy dishes like squirrel-head gravy, Nana Thibodeaux's dump cake, and blood sausage po-boys. No, a Cajun potluck dinner wasn't sounding like a great idea. However, I was in favor of serving a meal, because, after all, this *is* Louisiana, where people really just don't know how to get together with each other and not eat.

So we went forward with the plan for a churchwide dinner, but we decided to take the concept in a slightly different direction. Our idea was to bless people with a nice dinner, free of charge. We told everybody to leave their hog-head cheese recipes at home and just show up; the meal was on us. We bought what seemed like a ton of food, and three guys in the church served as our chefs. It was a huge success. People were excited about coming to church and getting a free (and appetizing) meal.[8] We were learning that whenever you find something that meets a need *and* makes people excited about coming to church, it is probably worth doing.

We were learning that whenever you find something that meets a need *and* makes people excited about coming to church, it is probably worth doing.

Word spread in our community about a different kind of church that liked to pick up trash, care for single moms, and cook free meals. We were gaining momentum in reaching our community, and as a result, our servolution was well underway.

SERVOLUTION STRATEGY

A servolution often requires innovation. This means thinking about who is not being targeted and who is falling through the cracks, then getting creative about meeting those needs. It means noticing who is on the bottom of everyone's list and putting them at the top of yours. It's giving and serving with no strings attached. And yes, that means serving them even if they will never set foot inside your church. If you will focus your energies on simply meeting the needs of God's people, you will never need to worry about the growth of your church. God will bless those who bless His people. Here are some suggestions to help you get started:

- *Pray.* Ask God to open your eyes to the needs all around you and to help you to see His people the way He sees them.
- *Listen.* Find out what God is doing and jump on board.
- *Believe.* Even if you don't have enough money to accomplish all that needs to be done, you can still start with what God has given you.
- *Act.* Roll up your sleeves and be hands-on in the work. Don't just write the check and run. Get in there close enough to the need that you can touch it, feel it, and smell it.
- *Give.* Give stuff away—as much as you can, as often as you can. Whatever you can get your hands on, give it away. Giving stuff away can be pretty interesting.

1. Where is God asking you to begin today? Which of these suggestions could be a next step for you or an area in which you need to grow?

2. *Attitude of serving.* At HPC, the attitude of serving is captured in the phrase "whatever, whenever." We want to be willing to do whatever it takes, whenever we are needed. What phrase describes your attitude of service?

3. *Identify needs.* Our servolution began by identifying the needs in our community. We looked through newspapers, contacted community organizations, and asked lots of questions. What are some steps you can take to identify the needs in your community?

CHAPTER 2

STRATEGIC SERVOLUTION
RAT BAIT AND CHEETAH-PRINT NIGHTGOWNS

We were experiencing the amazing privilege of being a part of changing people's lives simply by meeting their needs. We were like a kid who'd been allowed to have just one taste of the world's best ice cream[1] and was overwhelmingly determined to go back for more. A passion for serving others was burning in all of our hearts. We had been doing what we could find to do, whatever opportunities God gave us no matter how small they seemed. Don't forget the principle of God's kingdom: those who are faithful with the little things will be given much. We didn't know it, but our servolution was getting ready to explode.

It started with a chain reaction that ignited when our sound system fried. We needed a new system, but still being a very young church, we didn't have the budget to just go out and buy one. So we decided to hold a big garage sale to raise the funds. We asked people to donate items for the sale, and soon our parking lot was filled with our congregation's gently used, throwaway valuables. There were toasters, couches, pogo sticks, 8-track players, ceramic roosters, Ginsu knife sets, and other as-seen-on-TV treasures. I'm pretty sure there was even one of those Flowbee haircutting things.[2]

Just hours before the sale, I received a call from a man who wanted to give an offering to pay for the new sound system. How cool! The need for a new sound system was met and we hadn't even sold one item yet!

But now we had all this stuff sitting in the parking lot. Since it was all ready anyway, we decided to go ahead with the sale, thinking maybe we would be able to buy some new microphones and instruments as well.

Now, let me remind you my intent here is not to offer a formula for starting a servolution. So much of the servolution journey for us has been going with the flow, and taking advantage of the unexpected turns that we didn't see coming but God had been preparing us for. What happened on the day of the garage sale was unplanned and accidental. But looking back, it is easy to see that it was clearly God's plan for us all along.

We started the sale early in the morning, complete with food, drinks, and other concessions. I was looking forward to meeting all the new people who would drive onto our small campus that day. I was also looking forward to helping them fill their trunks with great garage-sale treasures. What I didn't expect was all the haggling that was about to begin. It wasn't long before I was no longer happy to see any of these new people. After about the fifteenth lady who tried to haggle me down to a quarter for a mauve and country-blue wind chime marked at fifty cents, I had finally had it. I walked over to one of the volunteers and said, "I can't take this haggling anymore! So I have an idea. Let's just *give* everything away—food, drinks, *everything*. What do you think? Can we pull it off?" I knew it could create a crazy out-of-control scene to do it without a decent plan, so I sent her off to devise a riot-free strategy.

I walked over to one of the volunteers and said, "I can't take this haggling anymore! So I have an idea. Let's just *give* everything away—food, drinks, *everything*."

Ten minutes later, her team had thought of the perfect plan. When people came up, we told them they had a certain limit they could take for free: up to five items or up to a particular sum. Not only did we give everything away, but we made a great impression on the community. Plus, we did it all without my winding up on the front page of the local newspaper for yelling at a little old lady who was simply trying to get a better deal on a goofy wind chime.

Here's what happened as a result of that day: everyone was excited about coming to a garage sale expecting to pay but leaving with a bag of free merchandise. Word of mouth spread quickly that there was a church giving stuff away, and one guy even called the radio station to tell them about "this crazy church doing a garage sale giving everything away!" In addition, our people were having a blast hosting this first-ever *free* garage sale. It was a revolutionary concept, and it was refreshing to our community. The volunteers loved seeing the expressions of excitement and intrigue on people's faces as they got to bless them and could not wait to do it again. The chain reaction of our servolution continued as people from our community began to see church in a whole new light and started showing up to services because they wanted to be a part of it.

Jesus kicked off chain reactions all the time when he healed the sick and spoke into people's lives. For example, in Mark 1, the Bible says that one man who Jesus healed "went out and began to talk freely, spreading the news. As a result, Jesus could no longer enter a town openly but stayed outside in lonely places. Yet the people still came to him from everywhere." One act of kindness tipped the first domino that tipped another, and in the end, people came from everywhere to meet Jesus.

GIVE IT AWAY

Our chain reaction continued after the radio station tagged us as "the church that gives stuff away" and we received a call from a local businessman whose company deals in pest-control supplies. He had a couple of extra pallets of rat bait in his warehouse and wanted to know if we wanted to give it away. *Give away rat bait?* I thought. But before I knew it, I heard myself saying, "Sure, why not? Thanks!" still a little unclear of what I was getting us into.

We had one faithful volunteer named Mark Stermer[3] who always showed up to church on his days off, driving his full-sized pickup truck. As soon as he arrived, we set out for the warehouse and filled the bed of his truck with the two pallets of rat bait. Now, you may not know this, but rat bait isn't exactly featherweight, and Mark's truck nearly dragged the ground under the load. We started by taking some to the church because to be honest, we needed rat bait at the church just as much as anyone else did. We had lots of church mice then, and we still do now.

Then we began an outreach that would have put the Pied Piper out of business. We visited neighborhoods, trailer parks, businesses, a few bayous, going from door to door offering free rat bait. We'd say, "Hey, we're from Healing Place Church. Someone gave us this rat bait for free, and we just wanted to bless you with some if you need it." It took a long, long time to give away all that bait, but we did it. Those who needed it were excited to take some. Those who didn't need it were still given a good impression about the heart of this local church.

Every single one of the volunteers was fired up! We found that the more we gave stuff away, the more stuff we found ourselves being given to give away. How cool is that? Who would have thought that distributing those two palettes of rat bait was just the beginning of a whole lot more free commodity distribution?

We found that the more we gave stuff away, the more stuff we found ourselves being given to give away.

We have a friend[4] who at the time was working for a ministry that served as a huge pantry for inner cities all over the country. He had connections providing him with truckloads of a wide variety of goods: pretty much anything you could typically pick up at Wal-Mart. He heard about all the giveaways we were doing, so he called and asked if we would want to distribute truckloads of these items as they came available.

I thought, *Well, if we can give away rat bait, certainly we can give away food and everyday household items.* He took us at our word and shortly sent us a semitruck of bananas. Have you ever considered how many bunches of bananas can fit inside a semi? I've counted. A semitruck can hold, exactly, a whole bunch.

We filled our cars with bananas and took them to people who needed food, but even after hours of this, there were still more bananas to give away. We called all our friends and asked them to come and fill their cars so they could distribute some. There were still more bananas to give away. I started to think maybe this wasn't a good idea after all, since the idea of a semitruck sitting for a couple of days in Louisiana heat would not be a pretty sight (or smell).

So we did something that for its time was innovative. At the spur of the moment, we called as many other churches and organizations as we knew and asked them to take some of the bananas in order to get them into the hands of people who needed a blessing. *Finally*, we unloaded a jungle's worth of bananas, and a lot of people in our community got their recommended daily allowance of potassium that day.

As successful as this outreach was, we decided if we were going to continue with these giveaway projects and grow to be able to handle even larger amounts of goods, we needed to have a plan:

1. *We organized.* We needed the giveaways to be focused and orderly, not random and sloppy. We weren't going to randomly throw free things at people as they happened to go by and have the stuff end up in the garbage. We wanted to target the areas and groups of people who would benefit the most from these goods.

2. *We included others.* We knew the value of having healthy relationships with other churches and organizations, and we learned very quickly that including them in our plans for these giveaways was a great way to start relationships with many of them. So we developed a list of contact people from various places whom we could call when we needed help with the distribution.

3. *We gave with no strings attached.* The goal of our servolution has always been to demonstrate the love of Jesus, not

to make people feel like they now owed it to us to come to a service. Don't get me wrong, we tried our best to be sure to tell them where we were from so they would know that ultimately it was God who was blessing them. But regardless of whether they ever walked into our church, we wanted them to understand that both God and our church loved and believed in them.

The goal of our servolution has always been to demonstrate the love of Jesus, not to make people feel like they now owed it to us to come to a service.

So the trucks kept coming. We started to get two or three trucks delivered every week. The more we did it, the more strategic we became. The first time we received a call about a truckload of Snapple beverages being delivered to us, we knew just what to do. By the time the semi pulled up to the church, our parking lot was filled with the cars of not only our volunteers but also the leadership of many other churches and groups—all of them ready and waiting to load-and-go. Cars, pickups, minivans, and even passenger vans were lined up, making the church look like a drive-through Snapple warehouse.

That summer, we gave away two hundred and fifty thousand bottles of Snapple and over forty tons of bananas. And the best part about it all was that no one worried about who got the credit. We didn't insist that anyone who took stuff from us come to church the next weekend. We didn't require any of the other organizations who helped distribute stuff mention our church as they gave it away. It was all just about helping others. It was the body of Christ in Baton Rouge working together to bless people.

Another important goal we had was for our entire congregation to be connected with what was going on. So when the trucks came in, we often unloaded the boxes of merchandise and stored them inside our auditorium. This way, people couldn't miss them whenever they walked into the church. There were stacks of boxes ten feet high lining the walls of the sanctuary. I thought the people needed to see everything that was going on. At the end of a service I told the people, "You see all those boxes? We're going to be giving all of that away this week and we need your help with the outreach. But if *you* have a need today, pick up whatever you need in the back; we've got some people ready to serve you. And while you're getting what you need, be sure to sign up for the outreach this weekend. Come back and help us give to others who are also in need." It was a cool kind of crazy thing to get to do.

The trucks contained just about everything you could imagine. We would open up the back and sometimes there were forty pallets of forty different items: Guess jeans, cookies, Right Guard deodorant, Listerine mouthwash, screwdrivers, chocolate Easter bunnies, toys, purses, shoes, socks — seriously, everything you could imagine. With a list like that, we knew we needed to be creative to determine the most strategic locations to target so nothing would go wasted. "Screwdrivers? Let's go to a vocational school. Jeans? Let's go to some high schools. Toys? Let's go to the children's ward at a hospital."

There was only one time that we opened a box and the contents left us all speechless. We were emptying a truck, and when we got to the final box, I saw it was huge and barely holding together. After quite a struggle, we finally maneuvered it into the sanctuary. I was standing with about seven or eight of our ladies when I pulled on the top flap and one side of the box fell open.

Animal-print satin spilled everywhere. Everyone burst out laughing. This was a box of cheetah-print nightwear! My mind started racing. *Whoa! What are we going to do with this? We've got to get rid of this before Sunday; God's gonna kill us with this in the house!* One lady said, "We can't give that out." Another said, "Why not? It's free. I'm sure *somebody* needs it."

So several of our ladies sorted through the collection of animal-print pajamas in all sizes. Then we took a team downtown, set up eight-foot tables, knocked on doors in nearby neighborhoods, and handed out fliers. Ladies began to emerge, and the area soon looked like Wal-Mart on the Friday morning after Thanksgiving. In a matter of moments, every stitch of the nightwear was gone. Let's just say there were a lot of smiles from the precious ladies we got to bless that special day! For years afterward, DeLynn and I would run into some of these ladies and their eyes would light up and they'd say, "You're that crazy pastor who gave me that cheetah-print nightgown!" And if her husband was with her, invariably I'd get the "Ooh yeah" smile and head nod from him.

We were all having so much fun as a church. Working together to unload semitrucks, handing out bottles of Snapple, and going door to door delivering free food to the poor — all in the standard Louisiana 150 percent humidity. But the heat mattered little to us because of the thrill of meeting the needs of people who were so grateful to be remembered. Everyone was involved because of their passion to serve others, and that generated an energy that was contagious. When people discover the blessing of serving together, you've got the makings of a servolution.

The more we as a church bonded in this common mission, the more others wanted to come and be part of the excitement. The church was growing so rapidly that in less than two years, we had outgrown our facility. We had been faithful with a little, and now God was entrusting us with much. Our services were going great, every Sunday we had visitors, and new people actually came back for a second service, and a third, and a fourth. Most important, the culture of our church was becoming deeply rooted in the hearts of all our members. We knew God had blessed us with a mandate to be a healing place for a hurting world, and our servolution was causing us to grow at a pace none of us could have predicted.

Thank you, Jesus!

SERVOLUTION STRATEGY

As our servolution grew, so did the importance of being strategic in our outreach. But the reverse was also true—the more strategic we became, the more our servolution grew. Planning, being prepared to handle growth, and learning where to focus your energy and resources are crucial to being a good steward of the blessing God sends your way.

1. *The motive for service.* When we give with no strings attached, it shows that our love is authentic, motivated not by our needs but by meeting the needs of others. What is the motivation for your service?

2. *Unused resources.* If HPC can give away rat bait, it proves that you can give away almost anything. What resources does your church or someone in your church have that they may be willing to offer? What are the resources you have in your church that are not being used? What talents, gifts, and resources can you begin giving away?

3. *Church partnerships.* Working with other churches is an essential part of strategic servolution. What are some of the churches and ministries that you might partner with in service?

CHAPTER 3

THE CULTURE OF SERVING

AN UNEXPECTED OPPORTUNITY

Servolution—like any successful revolution—isn't just something you do. While it may begin as an event or an occurrence, once the effects of serving others begin to infiltrate your congregation, your church, or your family, servolution quickly becomes who you are. It defines you and shapes your culture. In a servolution, you discover much more about yourself and what you are made of, and if you let Him, God will change your world by using you to bless others. In addition, so often your future depends on it because there are lessons to be learned before God can use you in an even greater way. Your opportunities to serve tomorrow can hinge on your servolution today.

Almost every American can remember exactly what they were doing on Tuesday morning, September 11, 2001. I was at Sophie's restaurant at the Holiday Inn on Seigen Lane in Baton Rouge. I was sitting at the second table by the window, across from one of our staff who had just returned from a mission overseas.[1] We were discussing plans for what was next in our partnerships in Africa and looking at some upcoming local outreaches we were starting. Favor for our church in the community was high, God was blessing us, the servolution was growing, and life was cruising.

Then the news about the first plane crashing into one of the World Trade Center towers hit the airwaves. Our cell phones rang almost simultaneously as our wives called us, communicating the same message: "I can't believe what I'm seeing on the news! A plane crashed into one of the Twin Towers in New York and it's burning. It's a horrible scene! I can't believe this." I could hear DeLynn's emotions pouring through her words.

In the moments that followed, the country realized what we were witnessing was no accident. Live on the news, America watched as a second plane slammed into the second tower. While we sat in shock, our wives tried to describe this heinous terrorist attack over the phones. Through the flurry of thoughts racing in my mind, it sank in that during the last few minutes, our world had just changed.

That day, four planes crashed, two skyscrapers collapsed, a huge section of the Pentagon was destroyed, and thousands of lives were lost. My mind reeled at the thought of how many families, children, friends, coworkers, and loved ones were suffering tremendous losses that day.

We decided right then that as a church we simply had to respond, and we had to respond now.

We decided right then that as a church we simply had to respond, and we had to respond now.

It did not take long for us to realize that we were going to need to be aggressive in our response. Because our entire nation was turned upside down, airports had been closed and parts of New York City barricaded. We had to be creative in our game plan. The first thing our staff did was put the word out that we would host a gathering to pray for our country that night. A call to prayer is always a great place to start in responding to a crisis. Tons of people showed up, all hungry to do something to help, and we encouraged everyone that we were trusting in our God for everything, including our security. Our servolution's response to this national tragedy began with a night of intense prayer.

Despite the FAA's grounding of flights, we were able to charter a private plane to get two of our pastors on the ground in New Jersey just forty-eight hours after the attacks. Mark Stermer[2] and Ken Spivey[3] met up with some of the people we were connected with there, and by Thursday afternoon, they were standing at Ground Zero. Mark called me and said, "You would not believe what we're seeing right now. I'm standing here looking at an enormous hole and the firemen are climbing in and pulling people out. I have a list of what they've told me they need up here."

He began listing the needs of the work crews: blankets, gloves, clothes, water. Because of our years of distributing goods, we had developed a great network of people, organizations, and truckers to partner with, and we began collecting items and packing trucks to make deliveries to Ground Zero. We connected with about two dozen agencies in New York who were responsible to get the items to the people and to the point of need.

Hundreds of average folks in Baton Rouge stepped up to the plate and served their hearts out. People took off work to help load supplies into donated semitrailers, and truck drivers volunteered their time to transport the loads to New York. Tens of thousands in our community drove to the parking lot at Healing Place with bags of donated materials. It was an amazing coming together of those rallying to meet a tremendous need. If you could have looked at our church property from a thousand feet up, I'm sure we looked like a fully operative anthill—lines of people carrying stuff from one place to another, getting the supplies ready to go. There were people everywhere, working tirelessly, just doing what they could to be part of the servolution.

Mark and Ken found out about a large Episcopal church near Ground Zero that was cooking meals for rescue teams and relief crews. We sent several of our cooks, along with many kitchen supplies, to help with this effort. After the first few days of chaos, when the city began get back on its feet, we partnered with several churches in New York who were providing counseling for traumatized residents. Our support of these churches and their work continued for almost two years. In addition, we helped build a counseling center that was shared by many different counseling agencies.

One of the ways we were able to make a unique Louisiana-style impression was through Cooking for Christ, one of the first ministries[4] we started at Healing Place Church. Cooking for Christ has a mobile kitchen and serves thousands of meals a year to the poor and hurting. We sent them up to the Pentagon for two weeks to cook for all of the government workers and officials during the cleanup and reconstruction. There were several other cooking rigs set up there, but the longest lines were outside the rig with our Cajuns and their iron pots, who were cooking up some incredible jambalaya, gumbo, red beans and rice, and even some étouffée. O yeah cher, ça c'est bon![5]

The servolution at Healing Place Church had just kicked into another gear. Many people who had never gotten off the bench onto the serving field found themselves rij70ght in the middle of the action. Hundreds of our volunteers gave thousands of man-hours to get the job done. If you hadn't known any better, it would have seemed as if the attacks had happened in our own city. The people responded as if it had.

We have always tried to learn from experiences we go through. The response to the 9/11 tragedies provided a lot of great lessons for us to build on. Here are a few of them.

1. Serving helps to gain the trust of the community. Many times leaders ask me, "How can I get the community's attention? How can we let them know we are here?" We have done this simply by serving. It started with a free garage sale, then rat bait, then Snapple and bananas, and then loads from semitrailers. Before 9/11, we had been a food and resource distribution point for other churches, but now we had become a distribution point for our entire community. Because of the influence we had gained from doing so much distribution of free goods to the poor in our community, we now had credibility and the trust of our city. During this national crisis, we became one of the largest gathering points for goods in our community; there was the Red Cross, and there was Healing Place Church. All the TV and radio stations would announce, "You can drop off your donations at Cortana Mall or at Healing Place Church."

Our servolution had grown to the point of affecting our community in a big way. People who were not saved, didn't go to our church, and didn't even know who we were drove up on our lot with a truckload of diapers and trusted we were going to get them on a baby in New York. One man just getting off work at a nearby chemical plant stopped by the gas station and picked up a six-pack of beer and two cases of water. He came to our campus to give us the cases of water and as he got in his car to leave, he downed the last of his bottle of Bud and hollered, "Now you tell them firemen, 'God bless 'em,'" and drove way. That's when we realized that we had started to earn the trust of a different part of our community than we had before.

2. We can have an impact on a much larger scale than we may think. September 11th was significant for us because we understood we could effectively begin to make a difference not only in our city but also in our nation. The outreach strategies we had been developing could be applied in a bigger scope if we would enlarge our focus to include other states and even other countries. We possessed a hope and a dream to reach the world, and now we could see how this could come to pass.

3. We should always expect the unexpected. It might sound a little silly now, but when our nation was going through the hype-filled Y2K scare,[6] we had come together as a staff to plan strategies in case a turn-of-the-millennium crisis did actually occur. Looking back, I believe we were impressed to do this because these plans were crucial to our ability to respond during 9/11. We had already taken the time to map out crisis scenarios and our proper responses prior to this tragedy, so when 9/11 happened we were already prepared. This was invaluable, because it meant we didn't need to scramble in the middle of all the chaos that comes with crisis to come up with a plan; we already had the basic outlines of many relief and response strategies in place.

It's imperative for us to understand the value of being ready to handle crisis. What better way to communicate the love of our Savior than to be prepared to respond with hope whenever people are hurting? It can be so easy — whether that hope comes as a cold bottle of water, a hot plate of jambalaya, or a listening ear and a prayer. But if we never stop to consider potential disasters and to devise at least a rough strategy for how to respond, then our abilities as the body of Christ will be hindered. In times of tragedy, the church should be the first to respond, and that requires a high level of preparedness.

4. The more we partner, the more impact we can have. The needs arising from 9/11 were far beyond what any one organization could meet. Even when those needs were broken down individually, they still had to be taken care of through many different venues. We learned how vital it was never to go alone in our servolution. If we had not freely opened our facility and connected with local businesses and other churches to coordinate our response and our relief efforts, it would have been a huge waste of time and effort. Sure we would have been able to do *something*, but it would have paled in comparison with what actually got accomplished when people from all types of organizations joined forces and served together.

5. Leaders need to trust volunteers. As the scope of our servolution was enlarging, so was the army of servolutionaries it took to keep it running effectively. I had to realize I no longer was going to be able to drive this bus by myself; I was going to have to believe in our amazing volunteers. Because there was so much to be done in a relatively short time, we had to allow a ton of volunteers to lead, and trust that they had been trained well and that they would represent the heart and passion of Healing Place Church. I was so proud of the people of our church; they excelled! This situation brought to the forefront those volunteers who were capable of leading many others. It revealed individuals' gifts and talents that I never knew existed, and as a whole, it galvanized us.

6. People need to connect to the need. I believe the closer we get to the heart of God, the greater the desire we will have to reach out to those who are hurting. Serving people is not just something we *want* to do; it's something we need to do. People discover personal healing through helping others. When tragedy strikes, serving helps to ease our pain, gets our focus off of our own problems, and brings healing to our souls. It is so important that we don't always just send a check; whenever possible, we also need to engage with those who are hurting. When you do this, not only do you help the people who are in need, but you also strengthen those who join you in serving.

> **Serving people is not just something we *want* to do; it's something we need to do. People discover personal healing through helping others.**

Kids Comforting Kids was one of the ways we did this during the 9/11 response. We helped join a local TV station with Children's Cup[7] to provide a program for kids in our community to fill shoeboxes with toys, school supplies, and notes of encouragement for the children of New York City. McDonald's added their support as they provided drop locations in each of their restaurants in the area. Teachers got their classes involved, and some entire schools had each student fill a box. We had gathered over a thousand boxes, and when the shoeboxes were sent, they filled an entire semitrailer. It was an amazing response that made each child feel compassion for other children and a connection with the situation and the people in New York City. Over a thousand kids in the New York area were encouraged by the gifts, and a whole lot of kids in our community were blessed by being a blessing.

7. As we respond, don't forget about "home." It's easy to become swept away by the intense energy of helping people on a grand scale—beyond the confines of your city. But at the end of the day, you cannot forget about your own community, your own church, your own staff, and your own family. While the need in New York was enormous, there were still people in Baton Rouge who needed Jesus, who needed to be served in a thousand different ways. We made sure to continue all of our local outreaches. We also continued holding services and talked openly about the crisis, being faithful to pray as a congregation for everyone involved. Our services were packed during those first weeks after the attacks—packed with people from our community who were dealing with fear, wanting to do something to help, or looking for comfort and answers.

With the 9/11 response still in full swing, we actually stepped up our servolution within our city because people's hearts were opened by the national tragedy. We put together a mobile version of the dramatic production *Heaven's Gates and Hell's Flames*[8] and took it into fields and parks in downtown Baton Rouge. We put the whole show on a flatbed truck and presented the gospel in a way no one in our area had ever seen before. As a result, hundreds of individuals crossed the line of faith. It was incredible.

The many things we learned during this time in our nation's history were crucial for what was about to head our way. Our church was about to experience its toughest challenge yet in our servolution journey, and had we not been so aggressive to serve during the 9/11 crisis, we would not have had the increased capacity to handle what was ahead. Our hearts were enlarged, our people were empowered, our processes were improved, and our troops were ready to be mobilized once again. But what was to come was beyond what anyone could have imagined.

SERVOLUTION STRATEGY

We believe that as the body of Christ, serving is not just something we *should* do but something integral to who we are. It makes sense that the church should be the first to respond to crisis and tragedy when it happens in our communities. And if we can be at the front lines of response locally, why not nationally and globally?

1. *Reputation in the community.* Serving with consistency builds trust and credibility in your community. How would you characterize the reputation of your church or ministry in your community?

2. *Global vision.* Every servolution is designed to have a large-scale impact. How far does your vision reach? Where are you serving locally, nationally, and internationally? Where is God challenging you to expand your vision?

3. *Prepared for a crisis.* We never know when we may be called to serve in a crisis situation. Do you have a crisis response plan in place? What assets do you have that would help in a crisis in your community (cooking facilities, shelter area, warehouse, counseling services, volunteer base)?

CHAPTER 4

SERVOLUTION is ALL ABOUT JESUS
FOUR WALLS AND A SLAVE

When DeLynn and I set out to start a church over sixteen years ago, we weren't trying to become a church with thousands of people coming to multiple sites every weekend. We weren't thinking about how to get book deals, product sales, or speaking gigs in churches around the world. We were just two people who had a desire to help the hurting people of our community and to serve those who were not being served: the forgotten, the rejected, the poor, and the lost. We really didn't know much about outreach strategy, we didn't have any of the helpful resources that are now available, and we had very few relationships with other church planters who could give us advice along the way. We knew we needed to serve, so we simply started doing whatever we could find to do.

We had no idea our servolution (granted, this was before it had a name) would grow to what it has become today. The outreaches we started in our community for widows and single moms were the catalysts for the many of the larger projects we are involved in today. The free garage sale led to massive giveaways, then to distribution centers, until our influence in this area began to affect other parts of our nation and world. Our servolution seemed to take a life of its own (as most "God" ideas do) and to grow beyond anything we could have imagined.

Our focus has always been on those not yet reached, and as we have extended our hands with no strings attached, every aspect of our church has rapidly grown. Our staff, our leadership and volunteers, our attendance—all continued to increase in numbers and grow healthier every day. DeLynn and I thank God continually that we are so incredibly blessed when all we have done is try our best to obey God's call on our lives to be a healing place for a hurting world. It's hard to believe that HPC has now opened two dream centers, helped plant many other churches, and today has some very effective outreaches like mobile medical and dental clinics, orphan care in Africa, single mothers' car preps, prison church, food distribution, homeless breakfasts, along with outreaches in strip clubs, bars, college campuses, and schools.

Our focus has always been on those not yet reached, and as we have extended our hands with no strings attached, every aspect of our church has rapidly grown.

Servolution makes churches grow. How does this happen? How is it possible for a church whose primary focus is serving and giving to the poor, the hurting, and the people who don't know Jesus to grow to several thousand members in such a relatively short time? We weren't even following any specific church growth strategy. We were simply about helping people. I believe there are several factors involved in the answer.

1. When we focus on caring for people, God takes care of the church. In the early years of Healing Place Church, when we were just beginning our communitywide giveaways, my father-in-law, Wayne Austin,[1] walked over to me during one of these outreaches and told me, "If you'll keep the church doing things like this for the community, you will never be able to build buildings fast enough." Deep inside I knew he was right. But at that time, we had not even thought of our first building project, let alone multiple buildings.

A few years later, I had a moment with God that changed me forever as God spoke this to me again. We were holding a prayer meeting in our facility, asking God to fill the room with the people of our city. After we had prayed a while, God spoke quietly inside my heart. He said, "Dino, if you will take care of people outside the walls of this church, I'll take care of filling it." We have done our best to do just that, and He has always kept His promise.

2. Servolution is about expanding the kingdom, not just our church. The second part of the answer to how a church's growth is affected by servolution is that it really isn't about growing our own churches. It is about growing the kingdom. This is a huge concept for us. Here's how Jesus put it: "'My food,' said Jesus, 'is to do the will of him who sent me and to finish his work. Do you not say, "Four months more and then the harvest"? I tell you, open your eyes and look at the fields! They are ripe for harvest. Even now the reaper draws his wages, even now he harvests the crop for eternal life, so that the sower and the reaper may be glad together. Thus the saying "One sows and another reaps" is true. *I sent you to reap what you have not worked for. Others have done the hard work, and you have reaped the benefits of their labor'*" (John 4:34–38, emphasis added).

We have seen this spiritual truth at work in our servolution more times than I can count. So while we might reach out to a neighborhood, rake all the leaves in their yards, and none of those people ever step inside our church, there are families who do walk in who have never been in contact with a single one of our outreaches. They pick us out of the other thousand churches listed in the yellow pages. We don't invest a lot of energy trying to figure out what outreaches we can do that will bring in the highest percentage of return in the form of people in the seats; we simply make sure we are active in our part of the sowing. We understand the mark of a great church is its desire to build *everybody's* church. There are many times we will do the hard work and someone else will have the opportunity to reap that harvest. But by the same token, there will be times when we will get to reap a wonderful harvest that we did not sow. That's what makes it possible for the sower and the reaper to be glad together.

This is indirect evangelism: if we will take care of the ones nobody wants, then God will take care of the ones we would love to have. If we will focus our vision to build God's kingdom, then He will see to it that our dreams and desires come to pass.[2]

3. Every Christian needs to serve. There is a third part of the answer to the question about how servolution affects the growth and development of your church. The growth God has brought to Healing Place Church has been seen not only in attendance. As we have been faithful to our mandate to be a healing place for a hurting world, He has grown us in ways we never could have imagined.

A servolution is not just for the people who are being served; every Christian *needs* to serve. Now, I'm not saying every Christian is bound by some quota or that God says, "Serve ... *or else!*" Not at all. I'm simply saying this: just like the physical body needs exercise to be healthy, every Christian needs to serve to be healthy in their soul.

Through serving, our staff, leaders, and congregation have matured deeply in their spiritual walk, in their marriages, in their finances, in their relationships, in their emotions, and in their personal lives. In addition, our influence throughout our community and region has increased as our servolution has broken down many walls of religious, racial, and economic prejudice.

Because of this, a large part of our strategy for fulfilling the Great Commission — to go into all the world and make disciples[3] — is to engage our entire congregation, including new believers, in some type of outreach. We know as people give of themselves to serve others, they are learning, growing, and experiencing healing.

Jesus utilized this same strategy with the twelve disciples. Much of what He taught them came in settings where they were all serving together. In fact, everything about God and Christianity is about serving and giving. In the New Testament, we never see Jesus hanging out, chillin' in an easy chair while Matthew fans Him with palm branches and Peter feeds Him peeled grapes. Every account describes Jesus living in an overwhelmingly generous way with His time, presence, wisdom, resources, compassion, and of course serving. He aggressively sought to serve humankind, even to the extent of enduring the cross.

Every account describes Jesus living in an overwhelmingly generous way with His time, presence, wisdom, resources, compassion, and of course serving. He aggressively sought to serve humankind, even to the extent of enduring the cross.

It started with Jesus' leaving the glory of heaven in order to come to earth and lay down His life for those He created. Check out what Paul wrote to the Philippians: "He gave up his divine privileges; he took the humble position of a slave and was born as a human being."[4] Jesus demonstrated His love for you and me in such an unrestrained way; how much more should we allow our lives to be a reflection of this love to all people in our world, including the forgotten, rejected, alone, poor, and hurting?

We are nothing. He is everything. He became nothing and served us as though we were something. He laid down his everything for our nothing. How much more should we, being nothing, serve those He considers to be something worth everything?

When we committed our lives as followers of Jesus, we received not only true and eternal life but also the very heart of God within us. That's the exchange God performs within every person. With his entire life, Jesus demonstrated this heart of serving. He put it this way in Matthew 20:28: "The Son of Man did not come to

be served, but to serve, and to give his life as a ransom for many."
When He moves into our lives, serving becomes part of our DNA.
We really can't ignore it or shove it aside; that would be denying
our own hearts, because it is now who we are. Being a Christian
who does not love to serve is like having a crawfish boil without
the crawfish. What fun is that?

When I look around at the congregation of Healing Place
Church, I am blessed to see the growth and maturity of the people.
I can see God's true prosperity, not just in terms of money but in
terms of family, health, and friendships as well. It is evident in
their lives. I believe this is because they have engaged personally
in a servolution. They weren't satisfied to see a need and hope
someone would do something about it, and because they have
enlisted in this servolution, they have found themselves energized
and built up on the inside. When we, as the body of Christ, serve
together, we grow together. When we express the love of Christ to
others, we ourselves are refreshed and strengthened.[5]

**4. Servolution reminds us that this is all about Him and not
about us.** The last part of the answer to the question of how servolution affects the growth of a church is that it reminds us that
none of this is about us; it's all about Jesus.

I don't think Jesus ever left a city in the same condition it
was in when He arrived. I'm sure there were times when He was
able to enter a new village relatively unnoticed, but as soon as He
began doing His thing — loving people, serving people — a servolution ignited, and He and all of His disciples were surrounded by
huge crowds. The world has been, and will always be, hungry for
a display of heartfelt giving. If service is pure and authentic, many
people will be drawn to it.

Healing Place Church has never been about receiving acco-
lades or keeping a trophy room just off the main lobby to hold
plaques and rewards for service. Actually, this is probably why we
have received some attention at times — because we haven't gone

out looking for it. We have found if we will simply focus on the serving part and leave the results part up to God, the impact on everyone involved is always the best. In addition, there have been times when God has cleverly positioned us to be in the right place for our next step in destiny. I believe this has happened because our eyes were entirely on serving the people around us.

A few years ago, a man who was a part of Healing Place Church and who was a detective with the Baton Rouge Police Department was tragically killed in the line of duty during a drug raid. Our entire city was stunned. This is Baton Rouge, a place where this type of thing is not commonplace.[6] I was given the honor of ministering in Detective Terry Melancon's[7] funeral at our church, and our staff and team of volunteers were ready and willing to help in any way possible. We knew that a large crowd of people who loved Terry would be attending, all of them hurting deeply over the loss, and we were determined to offer "five-star service" in every area.

Because of the hundreds of police officers, firemen, emergency medical technicians, and city officials who would be attending, we realized this occasion was going to minister to far more people than we had originally thought. Plus, much of the community wanted to show its heartfelt support for Terry's family and our law enforcement officers. As a result, the funeral soon grew into a citywide gathering that would be televised live. Suddenly, we had been handed an incredible opportunity not only to minister to Terry's family but also to share Jesus' love with a community that was hurting.

I was so nervous when I got to the church that Saturday morning my hands would not stop shaking. I felt a heavy responsibility from God to minister in this situation, and I knew the service was going to be in all of our local media. I had complete confidence in our entire team's ability to love and to serve the many people who would be coming, but I was starting to be unsure of myself. I thought, *I'll never be able to do this right. I'll stutter and confuse my words. I'm gonna choke and let everyone down and embarrass myself.*

I remember putting my head in my hands just prior to the funeral and asking God for courage and strength. I sensed Jesus speaking these two things to me: "Go and just minister to Terry's family; show My love to them. And don't let Me down; be sure to give the simple gospel as you speak, because that's what matters when it is all said and done."

Oh yeah ... this isn't about me, I thought, *it's about Jesus.* (Sometimes we have to remind ourselves of the ultimate purpose of what we do.)

Oh yeah ... this isn't about me, I thought, *it's about Jesus.*

There was a powerful presence of God throughout the funeral, and Healing Place Church was able to offer our love to the hundreds of people present by doing what we do best: serving with extreme generosity. We were able to build trust and relationships with our city officials in a very personal way, and we did our best to make every single one of them feel God's love for them as we honored and served them.

Reminding us that serving is not about us but about Him, Jesus used our servolution to grow us. Once again, what we did not know is how, simply by engaging in our servolution, by caring for our civil servants and government officials through this time of mourning, God was building the bridges needed for us to go to the next place in our destiny. We didn't set out to acquire it, but the positive media coverage, the recognition of our service, and the new relationships we formed with our police officers, firemen, and EMTs were positioning us exactly where we needed to be to serve during Louisiana's time of greatest need. Just one week after Terry's funeral, our state was hit with its most devastating crisis in history, and by God's grace, Healing Place Church played a key role in the immediate response to the devastation.

SERVOLUTION STRATEGY

As leaders, we never need to worry about growing our organizations if we have engaged in a lifestyle of giving to and serving the people around us.

"So do not worry, saying, 'What shall we eat?' or 'What shall we drink?' or 'What shall we wear?' For the pagans run after all these things, and your heavenly Father knows that you need them. But seek first his kingdom and his righteousness, and all these things will be given to you as well. Therefore do not worry about tomorrow, for tomorrow will worry about itself. Each day has enough trouble of its own."

—Matthew 6:31–34

1. *Making decisions.* When deciding on events or projects to embark upon, how big of a factor is the potential for direct impact on attendance at your church?

2. *Cultivating a kingdom mindset.* How are you cultivating a kingdom mindset in your servolution? Would you be willing to invest resources in an event if it led to growth for another church? Why or why not?

3. *Giving glory to God.* What does it mean for you to "give glory to God" in every outreach you sponsor?

4. *Celebrating.* How does your organization take the time to celebrate and thank God for the healing and growth that take place during events?

CHAPTER 5

HURRICANE KATRINA
THE DAY THE LEVEES BROKE

"I just heard that the levees broke and New Orleans is flooding," Pastor Steve Robinson from Mandeville's Church of the King said to me over my cell phone.[1]

"Well, we've been through flooding before. I'm sure the officials are prepared for whatever happens," I responded.

"No, Dino, you don't understand. It's *massive* flooding. The levees have been breached in many areas and the city is in chaos. The 9th Ward is under twelve feet of water, and downtown New Orleans is almost completely covered!"

It took me a few minutes to grasp what this pastor was saying. Hurricane Katrina had made landfall around six that Monday morning, and although the storm was intense and much damage had occurred, it wasn't as bad as had been predicted. In Baton Rouge, only sixty miles from New Orleans, we had experienced some pretty significant power outages and a good bit of wreckage from the storm, but we were now thinking we had weathered everything fairly well.

Then I turned on the television.

The media coverage was shocking: broken levees, surges of water several feet high crashing through neighborhoods, dead animals floating in the debris, people stranded on rooftops, and everywhere others fleeing.

I have seen serious devastation while on mission trips to India and parts of Africa, but I never thought America would experience the kind of devastation we all were now witnessing: loss of life, homes, jobs, human dignity, hope, and peace.

Nothing could have prepared us for the awful images flooding the airwaves, but there was one thing we *were* prepared to do: respond. Because of the experiences we'd come through in our servolution prior to Hurricane Katrina, Healing Place Church was in a position to serve the enormous needs of the hundreds of thousands of people whose lives had been turned upside down in just a few hours.

Nothing could have prepared us for the awful images flooding the airwaves, but there was one thing we *were* prepared to do: respond.

For a week, we had known this rather large hurricane in the Gulf of Mexico was heading our way. The nature of hurricanes, like tornadoes, is very erratic, so people in this area know that until the landfall occurs, you really don't know how you'll be affected, if at all. But Katrina was one of the largest hurricanes to threaten our coast in many years, and we understood that at the very least, she was going to cause serious damage. So as soon as her presence was confirmed by the National Weather Service, we had preparedness meetings with our leadership team to review our plans of action for various potential scenarios. We called and sent emails to our volunteers to let them know about our response plan and where and when they should check in to serve. We were in contact with our city officials, communicating that we were willing to work with them in the event of a disaster. I also called the leader of our Cooking for Christ team and asked him to order enough food to feed seven to eight thousand people, but not to get anything that would spoil, in case the hurricane turned away.

In addition, I contacted several pastors, planning our strategy for partnership in case the situation got bad; we were aware that no single organization would be effective working solo, and we wanted to link together to be as strong as possible. We jumped on the power of partnership, with each of us positioned to do whatever needed to be done.

The weather reports were projecting that sometime on Monday Katrina would make landfall near New Orleans as a historic category five hurricane. So a couple of days before landfall, there were both voluntary and mandatory evacuations throughout the city of New Orleans. Almost one million people fled the city and the surrounding suburbs, packing Interstate 10 with bumper to bumper traffic for miles. And because our church is right off the first exit in the first major city along this evacuation route, we were in a prime location to offer help to those evacuees.

During one hurricane scare the previous year, we opened our parking lot as a rest area for thousands of westbound evacuees. We provided snacks and refreshments and cranked up our air conditioning to provide relief from the smothering Louisiana heat and humidity. We also dispersed volunteer teams throughout the area to give away cold bottles of water to the thousands of people at gas stations and parking lots who were refilling their tanks or taking breaks from the drive. So this time, with Katrina, with even more people evacuating, we did the same thing.

We went through the weekend as normal; we had services on Sunday, keeping a close eye on the progress of the storm on the weather radar. We had planned to cook and offer free meals for evacuees after our church services, but by that time it was fairly quiet and there really were no people around needing a meal. We all went home and kept a close eye on the storm as its outer bands began knocking on our state's door.

Then, early Monday morning on August 29, 2005, the storm hit and southern Louisiana took a pounding with about ten inches of rainfall and storm surges reaching fourteen feet. Wind damage was severe—trees down, windows blown out of high-rise buildings in downtown New Orleans, and pretty much everything damaged in one way or another. This really was no surprise; the storm was too intense to expect anything less. We knew there would be wind damage and flooding from the storm surge and overwhelming rainfall. But we had no way of knowing the levees would collapse. And we certainly did not anticipate the magnitude of the unfolding disaster.

In a matter of hours after the call from Steve, we learned about the unprecedented destruction that Katrina had wreaked throughout Louisiana and Mississippi. Over 80 percent of New Orleans was underwater—in some places fifteen feet deep.

Over 80 percent of New Orleans was underwater—in some places fifteen feet deep.

The lives of tens of thousands of people who had not evacuated were now being threatened by flooding. People were running (and swimming) for their lives. Many were trapped in their attics and on rooftops, waiting for someone to rescue them, and many died in the heat from dehydration. In addition, more than twenty-five thousand people who did not have the means to evacuate were now trapped in the Superdome, a location the city provided as a last resort for residents. By Monday evening, widespread looting and upheaval were sweeping through New Orleans, and it seemed that everything and everybody was in chaos.

Tuesday morning at 6:00 a.m., the people of Healing Place Church showed up at the church building—our staff, our leaders, and our volunteers all ready to do whatever needed to be done. All I can say is that everyone did what they do best. Leaders began to organize hundreds of volunteers, and our Cooking for Christ team began to cook massive amounts of food. Teams went out to highways (now gridlocked with a second wave of evacuees) and served food to those stranded there. Other teams went to work preparing two of our locations to serve as shelters.

Some leaders helped coordinate a crew of more than four hundred volunteers to serve as chainsaw teams and sent them into the worst-hit areas so they could clear the trees and debris from roadways and homes.

In the initial days after the storm, there were many areas that were not yet open for people or other organizations to enter. But our crews drove up to the sheriffs and police officers in charge and mentioned they were from Healing Place Church. Because we had earned their trust by serving them at their time of need, they let our chainsaw teams in orange shirts go through the checkpoint. It was amazing to see how God had taken such a sorrowful event as Terry's funeral and used it to provide the access we needed to show His love to even more people in Katrina's aftermath.

One of our first priorities was to clear the city officials' homes and roads. They had more than enough to sort through during this crisis, and we wanted to make it as easy as possible for them to do their jobs. The New Orleans Airport was turned into a makeshift medical triage center, and hundreds of people were being treated there. Again, because of our positive reputation and good relationships, our team with orange T-shirts was invited in to serve alongside the military's medical professionals when even FEMA and the Red Cross were not yet given clearance. For three to four days, we had Healing Place Church teams serving as pastors, chaplains, and just plain-old grunt-worker crews that were pulling twelve-hour shifts at the triage center. Our people cleaned up trash, served people, consoled and prayed with people, and even carried people who were being brought in by rescue helicopters. These volunteers served tirelessly and were a shining light for Christ in a very sad and intense environment.

PRC COMPASSION

As I said before, it's amazing what can get accomplished when nobody cares who gets the credit.[2] I believe this attitude is what allowed the body of Christ to rise to one of its finest hours in the face of Hurricane Katrina. Because the staff and leaders at Healing

Place Church were so well-equipped to handle their immediate plans of relief after the storm hit, I decided to stay out of their way and focus my energies on keeping pastors and churches communicating and coordinated. It was clear to everyone that the job at hand would require far more than any single government, city, or ministry organization could handle alone. We were all going to need to work together.

More than four hundred and fifty Louisiana churches were already connected through PRC (Pastors Resource Council), a coalition of churches and ministries we had helped form several years prior to address social and economic challenges throughout the state. The Tuesday morning after the levees broke, I was in contact with several key PRC churches, and together we decided to call every pastor we knew, regardless of denomination or affiliation, and invite them all to come together to work on our plan for relief. On Thursday, (only three days after the hurricane hit) over four hundred pastors answered the call, dropped everything, and showed up ready to strategize our comprehensive response.

It was clear to everyone that the job at hand would require far more than any single government, city, or ministry organization could handle alone. We were all going to need to work together.

Pastor Larry Stockstill,[3] Pastor Jacob Aranza,[4] and I joined together to lead the meeting, and we told the gathering of pastors, "There is a tragedy in our state. Let's not worry about our logos, our egos, our styles of worship, or any of our differences. Let's come together as the body of Christ to help and to love people." Everyone jumped on board. From this gathering we formed PRC Compassion, and with the help of a local businessman, it was given a nonprofit status, giving us the ability to receive and distribute resources to serve our state in the aftermath of Katrina. Several of the churches represented that day allocated one or more members of their staff to help coordinate the efforts of PRC Compassion, and we all fused our resources and worked as one unit.

With so many churches involved, we wanted to make sure we were not duplicating each other's efforts and that nothing and nobody was being overlooked. Daily emails were circulated to everyone, exchanging information about the needs being met by particular churches and ministries. It was truly a prime example of each member of the body of Christ working as a vital part of the whole. Almost ninety Baton Rouge churches opened their facilities to become shelters for the tens of thousands of homeless hurricane victims, some (like Bethany World Prayer Center) housing up to eight hundred people at a time and other churches sheltering groups ranging from twenty to three hundred and fifty people. Every church played its part: some churches cooked for city workers; some focused their efforts standing by on the boat docks with blankets and food for the people being rescued from their homes. Some combined with the Red Cross and provided health services, examinations, and screenings, while others helped newly homeless people reunite with family members who had been scattered in the chaos. There were victims who had lost their purses or wallets and needed new forms of identification, some needed to be counseled through the emotions of losing their loved ones and their property, and some just were in desperate need of a shower. Whatever the case, PRC Compassion was ready to find a way to meet people's needs through the vast array of relationships it represented. It was beautiful!

Because my part was to keep detailed communication flowing between all of these pastors, I was meeting daily with several people. I kept them updated about what others were doing, then relayed their information. This helped to coordinate organizations that needed each other in order to succeed in their mission. At times, I felt like an air traffic controller, as I had to navigate through so many dynamics and altitudes of needs and corresponding responses. In addition, I wanted to make sure there were no pastors who were being left out of the communication loop or who needed resources but weren't being heard.

PRC Compassion was able to channel an astounding volume of resources and volunteers into the hardest-hit areas of the region and saw amazing results. Starting on August 29, 2005, and in the following two hundred days, PRC Compassion was able to accomplish the following:

15 churches were reopened in New Orleans

42 churches were being restored

500 faith-based organizations were networked

684 counselors and chaplains were trained and put to work

1,587 delivery trucks were routed

5,952 medical encounters were facilitated

14,092 volunteers were deployed and 490,379 volunteer-hours logged

2,853,100 people were served at relief sites

61,260,000 pounds of resources were distributed

While PRC Compassion was helping to coordinate the combined effort, Healing Place Church was in full swing to accomplish our part. All of our campuses were involved heavily. Our Annex campus[5] not only became the headquarters for PRC Compassion but also served as a temporary full-service medical clinic. Two of our campuses served as shelters, housing three hundred people for almost thirty days, while another campus served as a consulate for relief efforts for our Spanish-speaking community.

Our largest campus (Highland) became one of the three main PRC Compassion distribution points in our region for the food, water, and other relief supplies needed in New Orleans. In just three months, the Highland campus distributed four hundred eighteen-wheeler truckloads full of every kind of commodity you can imagine. Also, our Cooking for Christ team worked tremendously hard as we distributed over forty thousand free meals in the first twenty-one days. Overall, we served more than one hundred thousand meals, and also provided food for other organizations and shelters that did not have the facilities to cook but needed to feed the people living there.

Our Highland campus was set up strategically to handle people's needs as efficiently as possible. In one area of our sixty-acre campus, we were serving hot food all day long to hundreds of people at any given time. There were tables and chairs set up and many blankets for people to sit on in the grass and eat. Another corner of our campus held the distribution center, where fifty to twenty semifuls of goods were ready to be handed out: diapers, children's carseats, clothing, shoes, toiletries, towels, tools, toys, small appliances, crutches, walkers, wheelchairs—the list goes on and on. People needing help drove up, registered at the front, and explained their needs. A volunteer walked them through the distribution center and provided them with whatever they needed. We opened everything up at 6:00 a.m. and closed after midnight, and the entire time there was a steady stream of precious folks who were in great need in the middle of a horrible tragedy.

Words cannot describe how I felt when I saw our church—our entire church—serving so many people for so many days with so much love and grace. Our staff and volunteers worked tirelessly and generously despite the fact that they had their own families to support and tend to. Everyone had a "whatever it takes" mindset as they aggressively pursued this opportunity to care for the people who had lost so much in Katrina. They were not going to let this opportunity for a servolution slip through their fingers, and they treated everyone who came for help with the utmost respect and honor.

Here's an entry from my blog three weeks after Hurricane Katrina hit:[6]

I've seen some great things come out of the tragedy of Hurricane Katrina. Not to minimize the pain and suffering at all, but I've seen the people of Healing Place Church rally hundreds of volunteers and hundreds of thousands of pounds of clothing, non-perishables, water, and everything else you can imagine. I've seen hundreds of local churches partner together with PRC Compassion to send thousands of volunteers and millions of pounds of goods into the relief area. Through medical equipment, generators, chainsaws, thousands and thousands of meals, hours of meetings, dozens of chaplains and trauma counselors, cots, bedding, prayers, smiles, and hugs, *the body of Christ has been in the forefront from day one.* No single church could have done this — it was just the Church. To God be the glory!

SERVOLUTION STRATEGY

When we looked back at the effects of Katrina, we saw so many people in so much need. From the rich, to the "average Joe," to the poorest of the poor, each of these individuals needed the love of Jesus, and we were so blessed to be a part of the overwhelming response to meet that need. Mother Teresa once said, "Love has a hem to her garment that reaches the very dust, it sweeps the stains from the streets, and the lanes, and because it can, it must."

The spark of a true servolution is a simple desire to reach the world by serving one person at a time. Jesus taught us, "Whatever you did for one of the least of these brothers of mine, you did for me."[7]

Here are a few ideas to help you be prepared to respond to a crisis in your community or just to show Jesus' love to your community:

1. *Remember that you don't have to wait for a crisis to respond to a need.* If you have never involved your church in the smaller needs of the community around you, you will never be able to handle meeting those needs on a much larger scale.

2. *Serve the first responders* (sheriff's office, police department, fire department). Reach out to them now. Build and develop relationships with those who serve your community.

3. *Build a team of chaplains and leaders* who are ready to respond to crisis situations.

4. *Collaborate with other churches* in your area and learn their specialties.

5. *Identify emerging leaders* who will influence efforts with a kingdom mentality.

6. *Practice preparedness.* For example:
   - Serve now in community moments, whether painful times or celebrations.
   - Identify and leverage the gifts around you; there are more than you can imagine.

- Keep your head on swivel, your heart soft, and your hand open to give.

There are opportunities to respond to a crisis all around us every day—people dealing with AIDS, divorce, cancer, death, financial ruin, teen pregnancy, child abuse, anger, loss—the list is far too long. Ask God to let you see the needs around you and to bless you with the grace and favor to meet them. Also, I have included appendix 1 at the end of this book to help you with ideas for specific outreaches and how to make them happen, as well as appendix 2 to help you connect with organizations that are fully engaged in their own servolutions.

1. *First responders.* What kind of relationship does your ministry have with the "first responders" in your community? How can you reach out and serve them with God's love?

2. *Collaboration.* Consider two or three churches in your community. What are their specialties, the ways they are most effective in serving? How might you collaborate with them in ministering to your community?

3. *Community moments.* What are some of the "community moments" you've seen in the past year? How could you have served your community during these times? How can you prepare for them?

CHAPTER 6

SERVOLUTION TOP TEN
A LESSON FROM BEN AND JERRY'S

Every revolution has its defining moments. As I mentioned in the first chapter, the Boston Tea Party was one of the defining moments for the American Revolution. On that incredible night, the citizens of the colonies took an aggressive, proactive stand against the tyranny being imposed on them. They no longer saw themselves as a body of people unable to take action or too weak to bring about change. They realized that if they united, they would have the ability to free themselves from oppression and bondage. Although it took several years—tens of thousands of sacrificed lives—these revolutionaries eventually gained their independence. But it was on the night of the Boston Tea Party that they began to own their independence.

In our servolution, Hurricane Katrina was a defining moment for us. And I believe it was a defining moment for hundreds of churches in our region as well. As we grabbed the initiative, came together as a unified army, and responded immediately to the incredible need, we got a preview of the possibilities available to the church. We realized that when we work together, God gives His people an amazing ability to get an enormous job done. Our hearts were enlarged to understand more about the vital importance of the local church in every community, and how our influence and service can become an undeniable voice heard throughout the nation and the world. I believe there were churches that no longer saw themselves as a body of people unable to take action or too weak to bring about change. Healing Place Church and many other churches, through the experience of Katrina, began to own God's mandate for the church to be the hands and feet of the body of Christ. It united us and once again galvanized our entire congregation to embrace the ongoing servolution.

As a result, we saw clearly that Katrina was not the culmination of our servolution and that it wasn't the pinnacle for HPC. Rather, this experience was a cannon that shot us forward in our destiny as a church. We didn't say, "Man, we really did a great job with that. But now Katrina is pretty much over, so let's sit down and rest and talk about how great we are for a few years." Instead, we said, "Wow, that was awesome! If we can make that much of a difference today, let's be even more ready for the next time we get an opportunity to serve." This experience only increased our passion to serve others, and we became a bunch of people who thoroughly love to serve.

We did take some time to rebuild our strength—our people needed it. But while resting after such a huge amount of service *was* necessary, the people of Healing Place Church simply weren't going to set up camp there. We were excited to see what God had for us to do next in making as much of an impact as possible for the kingdom.

Reflecting on those several months, we discovered some things about the culture God has given us at HPC. We now constantly communicate these cultural definers to our staff, our volunteer leaders, and our congregation as a whole. However, I believe they are not just for Healing Place Church but are applicable to every church and every believer who wants to make an impact on the world with God's love.

CULTURE OF A SERVOLUTION

1. THIS IS OUR MANDATE

Our church's name is Healing Place Church: A Healing Place for a Hurting World. That's a big statement to put on all of our signs.

So if we're going to say it, then we're going to have to deliver it. But we know that this is why we are here and that it's what we are called to do. Whatever name your sign says, whatever your family name is, wherever you're from, if you're a follower of Christ, your mandate is to "love one another,"[1] to "love your neighbor as yourself,"[2] and to "preach good news to the poor," "bind up the brokenhearted," and "proclaim freedom for the captives."[3]

It isn't just for Healing Place Church. God has called *His* church (all believers throughout the world included) to be a healing place for a hurting world. It's the reason we started Healing Place Church, and DeLynn and I have done our best never to sway from this call. This is the heartbeat of everything we do, and almost every lesson I teach resonates with it. We do not approach a need with the idea that this really should be someone else's job. If someone is hurting, then the church should be the first to offer help.

When I was a little kid, I got a pretty nasty burn on my leg. The doctor applied over the large open wound a bandage designed to adhere to the burned skin. The bandage was made of a material that had a healing ointment in it, and as the burn healed and the skin began to grow, the bandage and the skin fused. It worked almost like a skin graft, and it was very effective in the process of healing.

This is a picture of what the local church should be. We are not to be a band-aid that provides a small amount of healing and protection for the hurting people around us, only to be taken off and once again made separate. The church and the community should be fused, working as a unit to bring about healing. Part of our strategy is to become a vital part of life in our region, not just to be a place for people to visit on weekends but truly to be a healing place for a hurting world. We want to be involved, to be part of the cure, and to be a resource for rehabilitation and restoration.

The church and the community should be fused, working as a unit to bring about healing.

2. WE ARE NOT LOOKING FOR A BADGE

We are determined never to allow the plight of those we work with to become a badge we wear, or to adopt a prideful attitude that says, "We are the *real* servants; everyone else better clear out." This elitist feeling is not healthy, and it's simply not a "Jesus way" of thinking. To think for a second that we are better than another church or ministry because of how we work with the poor would be ludicrous! We don't need to be recognized, and we don't need an award. We do what we do because we love people and because it is the right thing to do. We're all just people God loves, and we are walking together through this thing called life.

3. THERE ARE NO EXCUSES

"The problem is too big."

"There are too many people."

"We'll never be able to make a difference."

"We don't have the money."

"It's not going to bring into our church the people that we want here."

"We don't have anything to offer."

All of these statements are cop-outs. Just think if the churches in our region had had this mindset when Katrina hit. No one would have responded. The problem was way too big for any one church to undertake, and none of us had enough money to meet every person's need. But our state was a disaster, and we all knew we needed to do whatever we could. If we had hidden behind these excuses, the church would not have been the first to respond, and many more lives would have been lost. In addition, the recovery process would have been much tougher and taken much longer.

It is true that we cannot do everything. But we absolutely cannot let that thought keep us from doing what we can. All of us have gifts and talents to offer, and all of us are able to do *something* to meet the needs of the hurting around us if we are willing to let God use us. No more making excuses!

4. GIVE WITH NO STRINGS ATTACHED

We never want those we serve to feel like they owe us something. If we've left them with that feeling, then we have not done our job. We are determined to be like Jesus, who went about blessing and healing people freely. Freely we have been given to, and so freely we want to give. We even make it a point to remind ourselves that sometimes we need to bless someone without letting them know who has been doing the blessing.

This is a principle God taught me while I was in line at a Ben and Jerry's in the Atlanta airport. I was behind a uniformed marine, and for some reason, his credit card wouldn't work. Embarrassed, he hurried to his seat to get some money out of his bag. So while he was out of line, I paid for his ice cream. By the time he came back, the girl behind the counter had already taken my order and was handing it to me. Now, I really wanted to hang around and watch him find out that someone had paid for his order. And, well, to be transparent here, I should say that I really wanted to hang around and watch him find out that *I* had paid for his order.

God gave me one of those feelings in the pit of my stomach that threatened to ruin my experience with my pint of Chunky Monkey. God often speaks to me in the language of nausea. I knew I needed just to walk away and let it end right there. So I did. Maybe my exit was only because my desire to enjoy my ice cream was greater than my desire to bask in the glory of my act of kindness, but hopefully it was because I had learned that my motive for giving needs to be about the person I am giving to and never about myself.

Give without looking for the credit. Wait instead for the eternal reward!

5. BE RIDICULOUSLY GENEROUS

Most of us know the old Chinese proverb, "Give a person a fish and you will feed him for a day. Teach him to fish and you will feed him for a lifetime." As true as that is, sometimes we do just need to fry up some catfish, pass the Tabasco[4] and some Tony's,[5] and let the people eat it up! Being ridiculously generous is one of the most contagious things that can run through a church. We don't want to be known for our average generosity; we want to be a church that gives with extreme generosity.

We don't want to be known for our average generosity; we want to be a church that gives with extreme generosity.

Ridiculous generosity is exactly what we received from God. He's the perfect example of extreme giving. Look at the incredible exchange God has offered us: we get Christ, forgiveness, and an amazing life, and in return, He gets us. Obviously, we have made out with the better end of this deal, but amazingly, God doesn't see it that way at all. So in His unbelievable love, He wanted us badly enough that He gave His only Son to die on a cross for you and me. That's some pretty ridiculous generosity by anyone's standards. My desire is for the church to see the world around it with those same eyes of unconditional love and grace and to reach out with the same level of generosity. It's going way beyond what's expected; it's over the top; it's going the second mile — just like our Jesus did.

Regular generosity is tithing; ridiculous generosity is giving offerings and *then* buying the meal of the person in front of you at Popeye's.

Regular generosity is serving as an usher once a month; ridiculous generosity is staying after church and changing someone's flat tire in the rain.

Regular generosity is buying someone a turkey at Thanksgiving; ridiculous generosity is cooking and serving the full meal for the person next door who has been going through chemotherapy, and then doing the dishes afterward.

6. DO JUSTICE INTENTIONALLY

Social justice is a hot topic right now in our culture; it's becoming a cool thing to talk about in Hollywood and in the music world, and that's fine with me. But I'd really like to see the church lead the way in social-justice efforts. We hold the key for true hope and eternal salvation, and we need to be that shining light in this dark world. In addition, fighting social injustice has to be more than a Sunday sermon or just something we say we are going to do; we have to actually do it!

This is where it becomes vital that we stay focused, stick to our game plan, and be intentional. We have to follow through and finish projects we start. It's only in being good stewards of our resources and of the opportunities given to us that we can make a long-term impact for justice.

7. HELP PEOPLE BECOME OVERCOMERS

At the same time that we are giving with extreme generosity, we're continually looking to foster an overcoming heart in those we serve. We believe that when Jesus said He came to give life—abundant life[6]—He meant it just like it sounds. Several years after Jesus said this, the apostle John prayed "that you may prosper in all things and be in health, just as *your soul prospers*."[7] We want to help people prosper in their souls—to move beyond a culture of blaming the world, having a victim mentality, and being addicted to handouts. We want to see them replace all of that with the abundant life Jesus gives. We want to build a sustaining ministry that builds people on the inside, one that convinces them that their environment doesn't have to defeat them and that by God's grace they can overcome.

Every person wants to be valued and to feel like they have been noticed. When we serve people, we always try to communicate how important they are to God and to us. Serving people means coming in and putting a shoulder under their load and saying, "I'm here for you; God cares about you, and you are not alone." It's helping them to understand that God has a plan for their lives and that they matter. When someone who is hurting feels a genuine grace coming from the person serving them, the result can be miraculous. They begin to overcome their circumstances and hurt as they see the value God has placed on them.

When we serve people, we always try to communicate how important they are to God and to us.

8. INCREASE YOUR CAPACITY

At HPC, we are continually encouraging our staff and volunteers to get out of their comfort zones and to look within their hearts to find new dreams and passions. We never want to stop growing and increasing our capacity to serve, to love, and to be able to get our arms around the needs of our community. If we settle into the thinking that who we are today is all we will ever be, then we will never be able to increase our influence and our impact. New skills mean new and exciting ways to serve. New dreams mean new opportunities to make an impact in someone else's life. One of the greatest ways for each of us to be a part of the mandate to be a healing place for a hurting world is to take the time to grow in our giftings, discover new talents, and deepen our walk and relationship with God. The stronger we are, the better help we are for those we serve. If you keep increasing your capacity, you'll keep increasing your servolution.

9. BUILD THE LOCAL CHURCH

Everything we do points back to building the local church, because the local church is where Christians are strengthened in their spirits, souls, and bodies. It is where we come together to energize each other through corporate praise and worship, the giving of our resources, and the teaching of the Word of God. It is a place where healing and restoration can take place, where strong families are built, and where amazing, God-relationships are built. We are committed to growing a healthy local church, to be about building what Jesus came to build. Our outreach strategy, our dream centers, our global missions projects, and everything else we do are either about establishing or strengthening the ability of the local church to glorify God by being a life-giving influence in people's lives.

10. REMEMBER THE POOR

Psalm 41:1 says, "Blessed is he who considers the poor" (NKJV). This is our theme. It is a filter for all we do and how we do it. It permeates all that we say and how we say it. When we are making decisions for our ministry, trying to chart a new teaching series, considering expanding a campus, planning how to spend our budgets, I feel strongly that God wants us to keep this question at the forefront: How will this affect the poor? And we regularly evaluate ourselves using this guideline: How are we doing at considering the poor? And what have I done lately to help the poor?

These ten principles define our culture and keep us on course. By checking ourselves against them continually, we help ensure that the culture of servolution is being communicated — and lived out — by our staff, leaders, and volunteers. If you'll adapt these principles of servolution to your church, they can help you ignite a servolution in your community.

SERVOLUTION STRATEGY

Every church needs a strong culture that reflects the passions of the staff and leadership. The ten statements in this chapter have helped us to define and express our culture at Healing Place Church. Take some time to consider the culture of your church or ministry. How have the passions and interests of your church leadership defined your culture?

1. *Defining culture.* Which of the ten statements that define the culture of HPC resonates most with you right now? Why?

2. *No excuses.* What are some of the common excuses you've heard for not responding to the needs of your community? Are these excuses legitimate? Why or why not?

3. *Increasing our capacity.* How can you encourage your volunteers to grow and discover their talents and gifts? How are you helping people identify their areas of service? What kind of training do you provide for them?

CHAPTER 7

THE FABRIC OF A SERVOLUTION
A TOWEL AND A BASIN

On the day Pastor John Osteen handed DeLynn and me that four hundred dollar check to help us start Healing Place Church, we had attended Sunday morning service at his church. The building was packed with about seven thousand people, the music was amazing, and DeLynn and I had come anticipating a great message from one of our favorite pastors.

He had just started to teach when he did something I definitely did not see coming: he stopped preaching, stepped off the stage, walked over to a young couple sitting in the congregation, and just started having a quiet, personal conversation with them.

I learned later this young couple had recently lost a child, and Pastor Osteen had just noticed they were sitting in the service. He stopped everything to simply go and love on them for a few minutes. "Dodie, come see, the Espinosas are here," he said to his wife, and together they quietly embraced this grieving couple, prayed for them, and even lingered for a few moments as they talked with them.

Meanwhile, the other 6,996 of us were just sitting there on hold, watching. It felt like a time-out at a football game. It was as if Pastor Osteen didn't care that there was anyone else in the room at the moment except this hurting couple. I'd never seen anything like this before in church. I mean, this was a pastor of several thousand people taking the time to interrupt everything to minister to one young couple.

Something came alive in me in that moment; a new thought, a new dream. I realized that it is possible to be a pastor of a large ministry and still have the ability to care for the one. This peripheral compassion—the capacity to reach out and envelop the multitudes while noticing the tiniest need—is one of my favorite qualities I see in Jesus and one I have always wanted to emulate. It is the character and the substance by which every servolution is begun and sustained. But it wasn't until I witnessed Pastor John Osteen's example that I was able to see how it would look in today's world.

I realized that it is possible to be a pastor of a large ministry and still have the ability to care for the one.

PERIPHERAL COMPASSION

I can only imagine how the twelve disciples felt as they walked with Jesus for three and a half years and every day saw the kind of servolution Pastor Osteen displayed that particular Sunday. Jesus had the ability to be in a crowd of people and sense the need of a single person who was desperate to be healed, like the woman with the issue of blood or the man lying beside the Pool of Bethesda. Through His eyes of compassion He saw things others paid no attention to, and offered miraculous answers to questions no one else even knew how to ask.

Mark 3:1–3 tells about a man with a withered hand who was in the synagogue one day when Jesus was teaching. Everybody else saw him only as the guy with the withered hand, but Jesus wasn't willing to leave it that way. In His compassion, He couldn't help but call out to the man and heal him. But notice this: the man hadn't asked Jesus for a miracle. Jesus just poured out a miracle because the deep well of His heart was full of compassion.

Another example is in Luke 7:11 – 17, when Jesus was walking through the city of Nain and crossed paths with a funeral procession. He noticed the funeral was for a young man, the only son of a widow. He knew that without her son, this widow had no means of provision and security and probably would be kicked out of her village. He told the woman, "Don't cry," but He wasn't just trying to give her some comfort. That deep well of compassion spilled over again as He turned to the young man and told him to wake up.

There's something else in this story that I love. The Bible says the man immediately sat up and Jesus "presented him to his mother." How cool is that? Jesus presented this young man to his mother (whose jaw I'm sure was on the ground about this time), and all at once He gave her beloved son back to her and restored her hope for the future. That had to be cool to see!

Again, note that this woman had not clawed at the feet of Jesus, begging Him to raise her son from the dead. She was not even aware Jesus was there. As far as she was concerned, He was simply part of the crowd she was passing by in her time of mourning. But to Jesus, this was a divine appointment. He saw an opportunity to help a precious widow, and He reached out to meet the need. His act of service that day revolutionized one woman's life, changing her spiritually, emotionally, and physically forever. And think about the story times she had with her grandchildren over the years to come — what a great way to plant in their young lives seeds of faith in God and His love for them.

Jesus lived His life seeking opportunities to turn His love for people into action — everything a servolution is about. For us, it's seeing our world, our communities, our work environments, and our families through the compassionate eyes of Jesus. It's allowing Him to show us where people really are, what struggles they are going through, and to motivate us to activity. It's taking the time to stop our busyness long enough to notice the needs Jesus is longing for us to meet. Heaven sees it all, and when we connect with Christ, who is living on the inside of us, we will be able to see it too. Then, like Jesus, we'll be able to see past the crowds and embrace the need of the one.

Jesus lived His life seeking opportunities to turn His love for people into action.

It always goes back to the vision DeLynn and I had when we started the church; our hearts are to reach the world by serving one.

SERVOLUTION'S MOST POWERFUL TOOL: A TOWEL

Possibly the clearest picture of servolution I see in the Bible is in John 13. It's just a few hours before Jesus' arrest and less than a day before His crucifixion. He and the twelve disciples are getting ready for the Passover meal. Jesus is aware of what earthshaking events are about to unfold, while the disciples still really don't have a clue. Lingering in the air are the echoes of the dispute they had been having about which one of them was the greatest. Ironically, they were all just a few hours from fleeing from Jesus, scattering and hiding to save their own lives while He was being led away to lay His own life down. Greatness was still a long way off for all of them.

As they walked into the place where they would share the Passover dinner, Jesus heard their argument. I can't imagine how He must have felt about it. He'd been coaching and teaching these men for three and a half years, and they still hadn't let go of their pride. And now, He was about to leave them with the responsibility of carrying His message to the rest of the world! Thankfully, Jesus still had hope in their capacity to learn and understand. He took a towel from beside the basin at the entryway and tied it around His waist.

The disciples were shocked. Putting on the towel was a huge statement. Jesus was their rabbi and leader and it was culturally inconceivable for Him to take that towel and put it on. It was customary for there to be a basin of water at the entry of every home so that when a guest came in, he could have his feet washed. The dirt roads they walked were covered in filth (including animal dung), and since sandals were the only shoes available, people's feet would be plain old nasty after a journey. Having your feet washed wasn't a luxury; it was a necessity. But the guest would never be expected to wash his own feet; foot-washing was done by the least-paid or the lowest-ranked servant.

That night, each of the apostles had passed right by the basin in the entryway. They knew that since this was a borrowed location, one of them was going to have to suck it up and be the one to wash the others' feet, but none of them volunteered. It's easy to understand this, given the arguments they were having about which one of them was the greatest. Whoever would have decided to stoop and pick up the towel would be admitting he was the least-ranked. It would prove he certainly held the status of less than the best.

Then Jesus messed with their heads by taking the towel Himself.

John 13:1 describes the moment: "It was just before the Passover Feast. Jesus knew that the time had come for him to leave this world and go to the Father. Having loved his own who were in the world, he now showed them the full extent of his love." He carried the basin over to His disciples, knelt, and began to remove each one's sandals and wash their feet from the filth of the journey. Certainly, they all felt ashamed and embarrassed to have their master do what they were too proud to do.

Once Jesus was done washing their feet, He got up, put the basin and towel away, and then put his robe back on. Can you imagine the awkwardness during those few moments? Jesus broke the silence: "Do you understand what I have done for you?... You call me 'Teacher' and 'Lord,' and rightly so, for that is what I am. Now that I, your Lord and Teacher, have washed your feet, you also should wash one another's feet. I have set you an example that you should do as I have done for you. I tell you the truth, no servant is greater than his master, nor is a messenger greater than the one who sent him. Now that you know these things, you will be blessed if you do them" (vv. 12 – 17).

It's as if He's saying to them, "Look, it's been more than three years, and we need to put an end to this competition and pride. If you want to really understand this gospel, and if you want to be able to truly be 'great,' you all need to get used to being a servant. We're never going to accomplish any lasting change in the world if you don't choose to accept what I have just shown you; this is the heart of serving, and what I have actually called you to be are servants. I'm not giving you a *title*. A significant life is about a *towel*. Everything else is empty."

"I'm not giving you a *title*. A significant life is about a *towel*. Everything else is empty."

We have all had times when we have seen a need but have walked on by because we thought meeting that need would cost us too much; a loss of time, a loss of money, a loss of status or reputation, a loss of what we'd rather be doing. But Jesus doesn't see picking up the towel and serving another person as a loss of anything. He told his disciples, "Now that you know these things, *you will be blessed* if you do them." Serving one another is the path of blessing.

My guess is that the young men in the upper room felt pretty foolish at this point. I doubt they had any thoughts about bringing up the debate over who was the greatest and the best.

But Jesus was not done with His teaching; He needed to give them a bit more, something supernatural that would help them deny their fleshly desires to dominate and to be looked upon as great. He knew they required inner fuel to motivate them to actually do the work of the ministry. Jesus went on in verses 34–35 to give this incredible statement: "A new command I give you: Love one another. As I have loved you, so you must love one another. By this all men will know that you are my disciples, if you love one another."

From where we stand today, after the fact, we can read this and see how it applies to the sacrificial love Jesus showed by dying on the cross. But He gave this commandment *before* He went to the cross. I believe Jesus was choosing His words deliberately and wisely in these last hours of His life. When Jesus tells them in this context to love one another by following His example, He's not referring to His death. For the last three and a half years, Jesus had set an unprecedented example of servanthood, and this is what He was referring to. "The way I've lived, the way I've loved, the way I've cared for you and all the hurting people — you need to do the same. Just as I have loved and served you, you should love and serve each other. Serving and loving others is how people will recognize you as followers of Me."

Sure enough, we read later in the book of Acts that the early members of the church were called "Christians," not because they had given themselves this name but because the people who saw them in action gave it to them. They called them Christians because they were emulating the life and the service of Jesus Christ. Throughout the book of Acts there are examples of a servolution going on, causing huge uproars in cities and even reaching to other countries — all sparked by followers of Christ simply serving and loving like Jesus did.

Jesus' words, "Love one another as I have loved you," are the fuel for every servolution. When we look at the unimaginable grace we have been shown — that He loved us even before we knew Him — and we allow Jesus' unbelievable love to be unrestrained in our hearts — we will discover an unlimited fuel source for a servolution. If we simply remember the King of Glory, the one who sat on the throne with God the Father and crafted everything in the universe, the one who gave up all His power and status to become a servant to those whom He created, and the one who came to earth to lay down His life for our sakes, then suddenly it won't be too difficult for us to stop at the basin of water to pick up the towel to serve others.

SERVOLUTION STRATEGY

Obviously, Jesus is the perfect example of having the keen ability to recognize the needs of the people around Him, even when they were sometimes hidden. But we all can grow in our ability to have His kind of peripheral compassion. Take some time to reflect on the following questions:

1. *Missed opportunities.* What people am I overlooking who are right here around me?

2. *Blocks to believing.* What keeps me from noticing the needs of those around me? Am I too busy? Do I lack sensitivity? What keeps me from sacrificing my time and convenience to serve someone in a small, humble way, like Jesus washing the feet of his disciples?

Here is an example of the impact that the Jesus kind of compassion can have on another's life. It is an account written by Donna Frank,[1] one of our volunteer leaders at the Baton Rouge Dream Center.

We first met Laura a couple of months ago when she came to the Baton Rouge Dream Center. The children she had with her were hungry, scared, and tired. She was angry and bitter. They were all homeless. The kids were not in school. Several of them had untreated ringworm and they were all filthy. Laura wanted to know if we had any food and if we had a place where they could shower. We fed them lunch, apologized that we had no showers, and prayed that God would open a door for them, and He did.

A businessman in our church who has a business at some nearby docks agreed to let them all take showers on his tugboat. While they were getting cleaned up, we were working on finding them shelter. By the end of the day they were clean, fed, and off the streets. After several weeks and a few bumps in the road, Laura finally found a house to rent. It had holes in the walls, no electricity, and a problem with large rodents, but she moved in with her daughter and seven grandkids; all of them excited to be together and off the streets.

Laura faithfully attends our ladies group at the Dream Center and comes early every week to help us set up. While she is a woman of few words, her countenance has softened and her smile is an encouragement to other women who are struggling. She's not able to read the Scripture cards that are handed out, but she listens intently and enjoys the teachings and prayer. Her life is changing and she is quick to give God the credit.

Three days before Christmas, some families from Healing Place Church went to Laura's home to deliver some gifts. She jumped up and down and almost cried when she opened the first package; a beige, cotton blanket. She said she was so happy that she didn't know what to say. They asked her to open another package. Tears ran down her face when she unwrapped a set of pots and pans. When asked what she was going to make, she proudly responded, "Gonna cook us a pot of beans." When asked if she wanted to make ham and beans, she shook her head. "Ain't got no ham ... beans'll be just fine." After a quick huddle, the Healing Place Church families gave her some money to buy a Christmas ham. Laura couldn't believe it. Before leaving, the group gathered for a prayer of blessing and thanksgiving. There were hugs and tears all around.

As empty and lacking as Laura's home seems, this is the best her life has been in a long time. Her family is together, they have a roof over their heads, and, because of the generosity of some people she'd never met, she and her grandchildren had the best Christmas ever. Her lights are on, there is food in the fridge, and she has people in her life that are willing to help her. Laura will be the first to tell you that God is very good. She puts it this way as she pats her chest: "I got Jesus in my heart, so everything's just fine."

Christmas is about giving ... God giving His Son ... Jesus giving us salvation and hope ... us taking that hope and offering it to others. Laura doesn't have everything right now, but she has hope. And that may be the greatest gift that anyone can receive.

CHAPTER 8

UNLOCKING THE NEED

THERE'S A GREAT TREASURE INSIDE

I've always been fascinated by people who can crack open a safe. It's so cool to watch them (okay, so really I've only seen it in movies) as they put their ear up to the safe door and listen for little clicks and taps as they slowly turn the dial. What stands between them and whatever it is they are after inside (usually some big pile of money or a huge treasure of some kind) is just a little set of tumblers and the right combination of turns and twists. If they can figure out the right combination, they're in. They've landed the treasure.

Every community is like a safe; while many might look similar in structure, culture, and ethnic diversity, each has its own combination, its own set of tumblers, its own pattern of turns on the dial. We, as a local church body, need to listen to it, touch it, and feel it click in order to discover the unique combination of our community. If it is true (and I am convinced Jesus was clear that it *is* true) that the body of Christ should show Jesus' love to others through serving, then I believe every church should work hard to put its ear to the door of the heart of the community and listen closely as it clicks. Such a huge prize is waiting inside if we can just find the combination that will unlock it.

As you work to discover the code that will unlock the door for your servolution, there are a few nonnegotiables you should keep in mind.

Nonnegotiable 1: A servolution is about people no matter where they are. At Healing Place Church, we have been very excited recently about opening two new Healing Place Church campuses in Africa. And rightfully so. But we also know that a servolution begins at home. We need a servolution where we work and where we live. Our greatest witness is going to be in our own homes and in our own communities, on the piece of earth God chose for us to live our lives of service. And because there is a servolution at home, we also have the privilege of igniting a servolution in Africa.

Jesus Himself was the first servolution, the perfect example of how we should live and serve. When He served, hurting people were healed, sick people were cured, confused people found answers, accused people were forgiven—a servolution followed Him everywhere He went because He served wherever He was. And that's how a servolution works; it starts where you are, then reaches out from there.

The important thing to remember is that a servolution isn't about geography. It is not a question of how far away we can go on a mission trip, and it isn't about putting all of our attention on those next door. It is about people; people matter to God, no matter where they are.

Jesus was called Emmanuel, which means "God with us." While Jesus walked among the crowds of people gathering around Him, He considered Himself to be one of them. He's one of us. The book of Hebrews says Jesus was "made like his brothers in every way" so He could become the perfect High Priest for us (2:17), and that he was "tempted in every way" (4:15) so He could fully embrace the human experience and be able to intercede for each one of us. He lived among us, He ministered to us, and He was involved in every aspect of life as a human. He was one of us.

How does this translate to us as leaders? A servolution must be an expression of our lives. It's not something to be compartmentalized as only a church experience, a mission trip, or a charity event we hold for our community. We have to live it in everything we do, everywhere we go. The teller at the bank drive-thru is someone God cares about deeply. So are the guy who just cut me off in traffic and the waiter who got my order wrong. We have to realize we are all just people and our value is measured by how much God loves us. We have to place that same value on others. We need to see people through the eyes of God's infinite love. The waiter who gave me a baked potato instead of mashed is no less valuable to God than I am, because God's love is the same for him as it is for me.

A servolution must be an expression of our lives. It's not something to be compartmentalized as only a church experience, a mission trip, or a charity event we hold for our community. We have to live it in everything we do, everywhere we go.

I have to remember that the people I encounter might not know yet that God loves them. I have to engage them with a continual purpose of transferring that love to them. If I don't engage, they may never know. This means that right where we are in our every day lives is where our servolution must begin. And it must continue to thrive at home even as we expand the scope of our servolution.

A great missionary[1] once said, "The light that shines the farthest will shine the brightest at home." I believe God is allowing us to reach a long way around the world with this servolution because we have been faithful serving at home.

Nonnegotiable 2: A servolution is a matter of the heart. Have you ever heard a song that made you feel really sad? Or one that totally cheered you up? Music can convey an emotion or set a mood without a word being spoken. An orchestra or a band can perform in front of an audience of thousands of people who have come from different parts of the world and speak different languages, and each person can feel the power of the music. A compassionate act of service has the same power to engage a person's heart and emotions. I've had the opportunity to travel to many different countries, and whenever I walk through airports, business centers, and hotels, I always try to listen for English being spoken. But even in those places where it seems no one understands English, I still have the ability to communicate with people through a smile, a hand to pick up a dropped bag, or simply letting someone go ahead of me in line. All of those little things communicate kindness in every language.

But my servolution can't be sparked just by a simple act; it has to be a simple act of kindness. There's a big difference. If my service comes from an attitude of obligation or manipulation, the impact is much different than if it generates from a genuine place in my heart to be kind. Religious differences, social status, and cultural prejudices are irrelevant. Serving others with a pure motive says to them, "I may not know much about you, but I care about you. You are valuable to God, so you are important to me." When we engage our hearts in our servolution, it is amazing what kinds of walls can come crumbling down; barriers of race, religion, and prejudice dissolve to nothing.

My servolution can't be sparked just by a simple act; it has to be a simple act of kindness. There's a big difference.

In our second summer as a church, we had been given a large amount of kitchen appliances to distribute, and we heard about some outreaches being led by the local chapter of the Nation of Islam.[2] They were trying to help single moms and the poor in their neighborhoods by offering after-school programs and by cooking meals, but they didn't have the equipment they needed. We decided to give them enough appliances to help remodel their kitchens.

This act of kindness opened up an opportunity for me to meet with their local head minister. We had a great conversation, after which he invited me into the mosque and asked me to stand behind his podium and preach for a few moments. He told me there had never been a white pastor on the stage in this mosque before. Sure, it was just the two of us there, but we enjoyed a few lighthearted minutes together, and then we talked about our beliefs about Jesus. I told him about my personal relationship with Jesus, and he told me a little about how they believe Jesus was a prophet but not the Son of God. We didn't get into an argument or anything; we just shared ideas for a while.

As I was leaving, he told me that in the six years he had been in Louisiana, never once had any other Christian leader called him or invited him to lunch, let alone gave them anything. I thought, *Wow, what a bummer. This guy — who is precious to God — must have wondered if there was such a thing as a Christian who actually loved like the Bible tells us Jesus loved.* Now, this story doesn't end with some phenomenal testimony about how this man, and subsequently all the people in the Nation of Islam, got saved. (At least not yet, as far as I know. But then again, we might never know until we get to heaven what impact that "small act of kindness" really made.) But I do know — at a minimum — we were able to replace what was a bit of a sour taste he had in his mouth from observing Christians from afar, with a positive impression of the love of God at work in His people.

My point in all of this is that when we engage our hearts and serve from a place of honesty and love, with no strings attached, we will have opportunities to display the love of Christ to every person on the planet.

When our hearts are engaged in our servolution, we actually get to experience the hand of God reaching down into our hearts and connecting Himself — through us — to the world around us. For those who have no relationship with Him, He chooses to express His love and acceptance of them through those of us who do have relationship with Him. We are the hands and feet of the gospel, and if we as His followers don't serve people with generous hearts willing to represent Jesus, no one will. But if we do, we can be sure that God is with us.

Nonnegotiable 3: A servolution must engage the poor. "We cannot let them get away." These words thread through almost every area of my life and the ministry at Healing Place Church because we know that if our servolution does not engage the poor and those who have not yet been reached, we are just wasting time. We aren't building the kingdom, and we're not fulfilling our purpose as a church and as followers of Christ.

When I refer to the poor and those who have not yet been reached, I'm talking about "the poor" in the sense that Jesus describes them in Luke 4:18 – 19: "The Spirit of the Lord is on me, because he has anointed me to preach good news to the poor. He has sent me to proclaim freedom for the prisoners and recovery of sight for the blind, to release the oppressed, to proclaim the year of the Lord's favor."

Our understanding of "the poor" has to include any person in any kind of bondage or under any kind of oppression who needs the freedom of Christ shown to them. Certainly, "the poor" includes people who are living in economic and environmental poverty, but it is also the person who is an alcoholic (could be living in the country club or in Nairobi's Kibera[3] slums, or anywhere in between), the person hurting from emotional or physical abuse, and someone who is lonely, depressed, or stricken with grief from the loss of a child. All people in all walks of life can be this kind of poor.

Our understanding of "the poor" has to include any person in any kind of bondage or under any kind of oppression who needs the freedom of Christ shown to them.

So it's up to us to be like safecrackers and discover where the poor are in our own communities, what they look like, and what their needs are. Regardless of where they live, where they work, or what kind of car they drive, a family whose son is addicted to drugs is in need of a servolution. Hospitals are full of people from every walk of life who need someone to reach out to help them through, to say a prayer, or to cook them a meal.

The key is to be ready to engage. Like the priest and the Levite in the story of the Good Samaritan,[4] it can be all too easy to overlook someone in need. A few years ago I had the opportunity to choose whether to engage a need or ignore it. As much as I knew better than to try to ignore the need, we were all just so exhausted. I'm not talking about the kind of exhaustion a person feels after a long and strenuous workout; that's nothing compared to what our Healing Place Church team was feeling. It was day fourteen of Hurricane Katrina aftermath, and our staff and volunteers had been working relentlessly night and day for two weeks with very little rest. I had been giving and serving more than I ever had in my life: talking, meeting, and strategizing with pastors and city and state officials, ministering to heartbroken and dying people in the emergency triage center at the New Orleans Airport, and leading the Healing Place Church staff and all the outreaches taking place at our campuses. After two solid weeks of this onslaught, I was physically and emotionally drained.

It was about 1:00 a.m., and our relief distribution team at the Highland campus was cleaning and about to close up for the night in order to be ready to reopen in only five hours. As I turned the key to start my car, all I could think about was my family and my nice, warm, comfortable bed waiting for me at home. Thankfully, I would be able to get at least a few hours of sleep before starting all over again later that morning.

As I was heading down the parkway leading out of our campus, I noticed an old, dirty Honda Accord turning in to the church, going very slowly. It was dark enough that I couldn't see the people inside, but I knew they had to be hoping to find some help. I thought, *Hmmm, what a bummer. The guys have just closed and locked down all the semitrucks in the drive-thru relief distribution center. Well, we'll be opening up again in just a few hours; they can come back then.*

I went ahead and turned out of our parking lot, and as I started down the road toward home, I felt the Lord say gently to my heart, "What are you doing? Where are you going?"

"God, I am *tired*! Those volunteers are tired and we've already closed for the night. Those people can come back tomorrow." I tried to remind God how the system was supposed to work.

Seeming to ignore my selfishness for a minute, God went on to make His point. "What if no other car *ever* pulled in here for help? What if tomorrow and the next day, and the next, nobody else came? Would you still be happy you let this car go away tonight without helping them at all? Dino, you need to understand that these people are a gift."

Man! I thought as I made a U-turn and headed back for the church. *How does He do that? He just put His finger right on the problem and left me no option but to see things His way.*

I flagged down the visitors and asked them what they needed. They were hurricane victims, and they told me they were just looking for a place to clean up. They were heading for Shreveport (a few hours north of Baton Rouge), and someone had told them they should be able to find help at Healing Place Church on the way. For two weeks they had been trapped in their house in New Orleans by ten feet of floodwater. They had squeezed into their attic and lived there for all these days in sweltering heat as they waited to be rescued by the boats.

I told them the distribution center was closed for the night, but that I would open the church for a few minutes so they could use the restrooms and get some water. I told them they'd have to come back in the morning to get supplies, though.

They were so grateful and followed me in their car to the front of the church. I unlocked the doors and turned on some lights, and when I turned back around to help them in, I could not believe what I was seeing. Out of this beaten up rusty Honda, eleven people climbed out! They were like circus clowns coming out of a VW Beetle; they just kept coming and coming. Only these weren't clowns. They were the dirtiest and smelliest people I had ever seen in my life. I had never seen people as filthy as these. They had lost everything; the car they were driving and the clothes they'd been wearing for two weeks in that attic were all they had. I could not believe I was standing on American soil and seeing this kind of poverty.

As they all worked their way into the church, the last of the eight children was a little toddler. His filthy diaper was hanging down to his knees—a mucky, soiled mess from the thirteen days of survival. He was so precious, and the sight of him broke my heart. I thought, *Oh my God, I almost turned this one family away.*

His filthy diaper was hanging down to his knees—a mucky, soiled mess from the thirteen days of survival. He was so precious, and the sight of him broke my heart. I thought, *Oh my God, I almost turned this one family away.*

I knew at this point I couldn't let them just come back tomorrow for the help they needed. So when they all came back out, I told them we would open the trucks back up for them to get whatever they needed.

We drove our cars back to the parking lot where we had the distribution center set up, and the volunteers came over to see what was happening. I told them I was sorry; I knew they had just worked so hard to close everything down, but we needed to open it all back up for this one family. It was a hard thing for me to ask these guys to do because I knew one of them had volunteered all day and was going to leave here to go to his job for a shift starting at 4:00 a.m., and another one had come here right after working a full shift at his job and was going to sleep on the property until work the next morning; he had not even been home in several days. I knew they were beyond the point of exhaustion.

But thank God His strength is made perfect in our weakness. Their response was amazing: "Woohoo! Another family we get to help! This is great; we don't have to close up yet!" Then they hurried to open the semitrucks, offering this family whatever they needed.

They were so much more like Jesus than I was. I felt so convicted. Here I was the pastor of a church called Healing Place Church: A Healing Place for a Hurting World, and I almost sent this family away while these volunteers, who were at least as fatigued as I was, were practically jumping for joy they got to stay up even later to help more people. They recognized this one family for the gift they were. I thought, *Lord, have mercy; I need to get saved.*

For the next hour and a half, we served this family: feeding them, getting them cleaned up, giving them as many things as we could. They took bags full of clothes, toys, and food and somehow stuffed them into the back of that Honda. I watched as the little toddler's mom washed him off with baby wipes and picked out the dirt from his hair. He was so happy to be clean and to put on a brand-new baby-blue onesie. He waddled by me giggling and smelling of baby powder and lotion. There's nothing like the smell of a freshly bathed baby.

The family was so refreshed and grateful for the help. After they drove away and we closed everything up again, I sat back down in my car in the dark and put my head on the steering wheel and prayed, "Thank You, Jesus, for helping us not miss this tonight." At least for those few minutes, we got it right.

When I think about the entirety of what we saw during Hurricane Katrina and the aftermath, this story marked me most deeply. The experience reminded me we never fully grasp the opportunity or the need that is presented to us — how significant a diaper, some baby powder, and a new onesie can be in someone's life. And that night probably did more in my heart than it did for them. I was reminded that sometimes serving is very inconvenient, and sometimes the cost of time, energy, and emotion seems too great, but in the end, the reward and fulfillment of serving completely overwhelm and outweigh the cost.

A servolution costs those who ignite it. I realize that until this point of the book, I haven't discussed the price and the sacrifice servolutionaries must be prepared to pay. I wish I could tell you otherwise, but the truth is every revolution has a price. It's a kingdom principle. You and I were bought with a price, and what a tremendous price that was. Since Jesus was willing to lay down His life for people like you and me, I think it is important that we understand we should be willing to pay any price to do something great for God. Any price we may have to pay is microscopic compared with the one Christ paid.

A servolution costs those who ignite it.

I included this story about the family who stopped by after we closed because I want you to know that even though I have committed my life to promoting the cause of serving the poor, I struggled that night with a strong desire to ignore their need and walk away. I'm convinced we all feel that way sooner or later; at least everyone I know who is doing anything significant for Jesus has felt this way many times. This is because it is inconvenient to help people. It's tiring to serve those in need. It's emotionally taxing to pour out your heart ministering to the needs of people. It's so much easier to turn a blind eye or act like you didn't see the need, to not get involved, or even to just send the check. I understand that feeling; we all feel that way sometimes. The important thing is that we not surrender to those feelings but pick up a towel and serve anyway. The reward is far greater than the cost.

Before I saw the family in the Honda that night, I couldn't imagine anything that could have made me turn my car around.

My bed was waiting for me, and I wanted to get some sleep. I felt like I deserved that sleep; I had been giving of myself beyond anything I had ever done and had been ridiculously generous with my time and my resources. Certainly I had done my part. As far as I was concerned, I had done far more than my share of giving. On that side of the encounter, I felt justified turning those people away.

I often think about the atrocious condition those children were in and the terrible things they'd survived. I remember the great relief and gratitude on the faces of those parents, and the smile on that toddler's face knowing he had a full belly and a clean bottom for the first time in two weeks. I'm so glad God was able to make me turn my car around. He allowed me to see that giving and serving people — no matter the time or the cost — is always a gift.

If we will engage the needs God allows us to see, He will show up and do something that never would have happened if we had just gone along our way and ignored the need. Life is so much fuller and more significant when we spend it engaging others around us.

SERVOLUTION STRATEGY

Every community is like a safe; while many look similar in structure, culture, and ethnic diversity, each has its own combination, its own set of tumblers, its own pattern of turns on the dial.

The following questions will help you "crack" the combination of your community:

1. *Demographics.* What are the demographics of my community? Who are we serving well? Who are we missing? How can we reach those we are missing?

2. *Influence.* Is there any area of our city where we feel we are lacking a presence or an influence? How can we help meet the needs of the people in those areas?

3. *Breaking down walls.* Is our organization comfortable reaching out to those who don't look like us, speak like us, or even believe like us? How can we reach out to break down walls of separation?

4. *Reaching the poor.* Who are "the poor" in our community? What are their needs and what do they look like? Who are we overlooking because their "poor" doesn't look obvious? How can we reach out to these people?

CHAPTER 9

STAYING on COURSE
A SPEECH, A SPOTLIGHT, AND A SEASON

"Dino, there is someone from a white house on the phone for you."

My mother-in-law, Dee Austin, handed me the phone. It was an evening in early February 2004, and I was watching television in the living room at DeLynn's parents' house. It took only a few seconds of conversation to learn this was *the* White House, and the man on the other end was Jim Towey, who was at the time the director of the White House Office of Faith-Based and Community Initiatives under the George W. Bush administration. After I picked myself up off the floor, I found the handset I had dropped and stammered something like, "What can I do for you?" The man proceeded to tell me that the president wanted to know more about Healing Place Church's outreach to people with destructive addictions.

As a church, we had recognized the huge problems with drug and alcohol abuse in our state, particularly in the capital region. We couldn't (and honestly didn't want to) hide from or ignore this problem, so we started to reach out to people in our community who were affected by destructive addictions. We began a meeting every Friday night for those who needed support fighting drug addiction, and over time, this outreach grew. A young couple offered to serve as full-time volunteers, and the ministry really began to take off. Then the media in our region decided to produce some pieces focusing on how faith-based organizations were tackling this crisis, and Healing Place Church's outreach was featured in these articles and news spots.

This was how we showed up on the radar of some of the White House staff as they were preparing the State of the Union Address. The president wanted to recognize this issue in the speech as well as comment on how faith-based organizations around the nation were becoming part of the solution. Out of several thousand news stories, the White House had narrowed the search down to about two hundred programs, then twenty, and finally down to our church and a couple of other organizations.

So there I was, talking to Jim Towey from the White House. He asked me a ton of questions about what we were doing, and I filled him in on the details of the program and the couple who led it. He was very kind and told us they would need to do a complete background check on this couple and me and would call again if anything progressed.

A few days later, I received another call informing us we had been cleared and selected, along with five others to be mentioned in the State of the Union Address. They asked if we could send two people to sit in the audience and represent Healing Place Church that evening. We agreed and were very excited to hear what the president would actually say. (To be honest, I didn't think he would really say anything about us, but I was still pretty excited about the whole thing.)

On the night of the address, when President Bush came to this section of his speech, he began talking about drug addiction and the people being helped by faith-based organizations that were working to make a difference. Then he chose to mention the name of only one church—ours! He said, "One of these is found at Healing Place Church in Baton Rouge, Louisiana."

I was shocked! As I picked myself up off the floor again, I couldn't believe he said it. And even now when I look back, I still cannot believe he said it. It's not like we have one of those safe, churchy names like First Church of the Denomination. Normally, our kind of nontraditional church would not be singled out in a national political arena like this. But for whatever reason God had in mind, President Bush did mention us, and let me tell you, we had no idea of the upheaval this would bring.

Almost immediately, we were bombarded by the media and other organizations wanting to know about our church and the programs we offered. In the first three days, we were contacted by more than seventy news sources, hundreds of churches, and many other interested groups from all over the nation. And for the next several weeks we continued to hear from the media all over the world. We even had a few from as far away as China and South America just show up at our church. It was crazy!

There's no denying I was tempted to think, *Wow. This is it. This is how we are going to be known around the world. By next week, I'll be meeting with Billy Graham and leaders from other nations. And after that I'll write a book and I'm sure I'll get on* Fox and Friends. *Shoot, I'll even get on* SportsCenter. *It's all just gonna blow up huge.* Dreams of all the influence Healing Place Church was going to have now and of all of the ministries that were going to spring up because of this were a little overwhelming for a guy who grew up surfing in Myrtle Beach, South Carolina.

DON'T TOUCH IT

Then just a couple of days after the State of the Union Address, I was at a morning prayer meeting holding communion in my hand, and I felt God quietly tug at my heart: "You're not ready to take communion; you need to examine your heart." And when I looked into my heart, all I could see was a great big pile of pride and ego. Then I felt like the Lord said, "Don't you dare think this is about you. This has nothing to do with you. Don't touch it. Don't touch My glory. You can't handle My glory. Keep doing what you are doing, but don't ride in this chariot. It's not your chariot." It was brutal to hear the Lord saying those words to me, but I am very glad He did, and I'm especially glad they came so quickly after those seeds of pride and ego had sprung up.

After I took care of my heart, I immediately expressed to our staff, our leadership teams, and our church that we could not let this whirlwind of media attention become anything to us beyond what it actually was: God shining a light on one church out of many who were making a difference for Him in this world. And that was it. It was all about God. *He* was the source. He was the one making the true change in people's lives. He was the real deal. We were merely the servants. We were not going to start signing off our emails with "HPC—the church President Bush talked about" or make T-shirts that said "George ♥s HPC." This was in no way going to become our identity; it was just something cool that God allowed to happen to Healing Place Church. We learned quickly to deal with the media attention, not to hide from it but rather, in it all, to ensure that our communication pointed everything we were doing back to Christ. Our servolution had to be a compass that always pointed to true north: Jesus Christ.

Our servolution had to be a compass that always pointed to true north: Jesus Christ.

It was a wild ride for those few months, and in the end, after laying down our egos and making a commitment not to hold on to all the attention too tightly, I hope we passed the test. The funny thing is that the dreams I envisioned that night during my rock 'n' roll fantasy head-trip were so much smaller than what God has allowed us to become just a few years later. Today, we are going far beyond that influence and receiving more opportunities than I could have imagined that day. I think it's because rather than allowing that bright spotlight to manage us, we (by the grace of God) managed it. Rather than letting it use us, we used it to glorify what God was doing through us as we stayed true to our servolution to the poor and the hurting.

STAYING ON COURSE

Many churches or businesses may never have the opportunity to be in a national spotlight, but most of us will experience the test of being given positive attention. No matter the size of the spotlight, as the opportunity for servolution grows, so does the attention. And as a result, we must continually check our hearts to make sure our motives stay pure. Whether we act on it publicly or think it privately, we are in trouble if we begin to believe we are the best at what we are doing or that nobody can compare to us or that no one is doing it as well as us. Lord, help us!

We strive for excellence, celebrate the "wins," and rejoice that God is working through us. But we can never take on an elitist attitude. It would be the beginning of the end. God's favor would be gone, I'm sure. So here are some ways we keep ourselves in check.

1. Everything about our servolution must point to Christ. All of our outreaches, all of our services, and all of our events must have a kingdom mindset—a focus on eternity. We are not simply a humanitarian relief agency. We don't serve and give only to improve the quality of people's lives, nor are we generous for generosity's sake. We give and serve with the purpose of showing people the hope they can find in Jesus. It's generosity driven by eternity—doing all we can to plunder hell and populate heaven. We want everything we say to point people to a journey toward Jesus. We want that for us as a body, as well as for each of us as individuals; everything we say and do must point others toward Jesus.

This is why we champion the cause of the local church. As much as possible, when we serve people, we want them to know who and what is behind the service. And because this servolution is about Jesus and not just Healing Place Church, we do all we can to partner with other churches who are already leading (or who want to begin to lead) successful community outreaches. We look for opportunities to help build up and strengthen other churches in our communities because we know that when we work together to show Jesus to a community, we collectively are increasing the spiritual appetite for Him in the entire area. A church never needs to be afraid of there being too many successful churches in their community. It's the same concept you can see at work with McDonald's and Burger King—when one opens on a street corner, often the other is on its way too.

So as much as possible, when we are in the community serving, we have our Healing Place Church *SERVE* T-shirts on and we tell people, "Hey, we're from Healing Place Church, and we're here to share God's love with you." But if we're partnering with another church, we'll say, "Hey, we're here with The Life Church," or, "We're here with Celebration Church and we want to serve you today." We know it is a good idea to give the people we serve a clear path to find out more about Jesus and about the local church. The only lasting change in a person's life comes from a relationship with Christ.

2. A servolution has to say no to good ideas in favor of saying yes to the God idea. As a church, we must avoid getting ahead of God's vision for us. We cannot solve every problem alone, and no matter how good the idea, no matter how great the need, we can't possibly do everything. We have neither the resources, the manpower, nor the ability—only God does. Given our desire to help as many people as possible through our servolution, we sometimes find it hard to say no to anything. But because not all outreach ideas are in step with what we are doing at Healing Place Church, we need to have the discernment to allow some opportunities to pass us by. In many instances, we have seen another organization handling an outreach extremely well in an area we had not tapped into, and rather than try to copy it, we have come alongside them as a support to help them experience even greater success. What was a "God idea" for them was a "good idea" but not a "God idea" for us.

What was a "God idea" for them was a "good idea" but not a "God idea" for us.

3. **Some outreaches are just for a season.** Once we begin an outreach and experience good results, we need to understand it may be just for a season. We started out visiting widows, saw good fruit from it, and today we still serve a whole lot of widows. But during the same time, we had a lot of opportunity to serve single moms by helping them move. We saw a lot of lives changed by doing that then, but today we don't seem to see as much of this opportunity. And we're not struggling to create those opportunities; we realize that it was simply something God had us doing just for that season.

There have been many things we have done over the years — wonderful ideas producing wonderful fruit — but we are no longer involved in them at the same level today. For example, we distributed a lot of truckloads of food and supplies, and it was awesome and we saw some very exciting results. But being a relay for commodities and handling that degree of massive distribution is something we don't do in the same way now. We developed systems that still allow us to distribute large quantities of goods, but they look much different than our original unload-a-semi-into-the-sanctuary system.

Sometimes a season of involvement in an outreach will end because a better way is developed to meet the need or the need changes. We must be sensitive to the fluid nature of our community's needs and continually adjust our outreach to stay effective. We cannot expect that what worked well yesterday will be the best way to meet the need today.

4. **We need to do our part in the servolution and leave the rest to God.** We are not alone in our servolution; the God of the universe knows and understands the person we are serving way better than

we do. He is the one who is seeking them, pursuing them, and drawing them. Our servolution can't save anybody; it's just there to introduce people to the love of Jesus and to draw upon the work God is already doing in that person's life. We are only part of the equation. This is great news because it means that we can give with no strings attached. We can simply do our part and then trust that God will take care of the rest.

> **Our servolution can't save anybody; it's just there to introduce people to the love of Jesus and to draw upon the work God is already doing in that person's life.**

Don't get me wrong; we keep our hearts alert for opportunities to give people a chance to give their lives to Jesus. If someone is ready to make that step, we want to be there with them as they make it. That's always a huge thing to get to be a part of. But it is not the only way we consider an outreach a success.

There have been times when we look back at an outreach and there didn't seem to be any tangible fruit from it. We might be tempted to say, "Well, *that* didn't work and was a waste of time, energy, and money," but I've learned not to think this way. If an outreach doesn't go as well as we had hoped, we may decide not to do that outreach again or not to do it the same way, but I would never go as far as to say that God didn't use it. Who knows? The next Billy Graham may have been brought a step closer to his destiny through the outreach. We don't know what incredible things God is doing in His master plan.

SERVOLUTION STRATEGY

Because there is so much need in the world, it is easy to veer off the course God has given you. Knowing the difference between good ideas and "God ideas" is crucial. Here are some questions to consider as you reflect on your own strategy for a servolution.

1. *Stick to the plan.* How has God uniquely positioned your organization to make a difference in your community? Are you spending the majority of your time and resources fulfilling this God-given plan?

2. *Learn to say no.* When you scan your organization's outreaches, are there any that do not seem to be in your niche? If so, why are you doing them?

3. *Just for a season.* Are you still investing energy into outreaches that once were successful but have become irrelevant to your community? If so, where might God be calling you to redirect your resources and talents?

CHAPTER 10

THE COST OF A SERVOLUTION
MORE THAN MONEY

Servolution always costs. Whether it's finances, time, energy, or manpower, every outreach and every act of service has a price tag. Serving our community has certainly cost us financially. There was a cost for the roses we gave that first widow, and there is a cost associated with serving three hundred widows each week now. We have made significant financial investments in our dream centers and our two international campuses.

While we believe every church is mandated to serve their community, we also believe that each church must be good stewards of their resources. We talk about this all the time at HPC. We've found that as the magnitude of our outreaches increases, so does the cost. Throughout the years, we have had to ask ourselves some tough budget questions. Otherwise, we could have become so excited about our servolution that we would have found ourselves completely in the red. So we asked, Does an outreach have to result in people coming to our church for us to consider it worthwhile? How will we gauge the success of an outreach? It didn't take us long to realize we had some decisions to make about the goals and purposes of every one of our outreaches.

As a church, we decided that sometimes the focus of our budget will be to host events that spur an excitement to come to our church, but at other times the focus of our budget will be simply to serve people, regardless of whether they ever come to one of our services. Our heart is for people to encounter the hope and love of Jesus, but whether they come to our church or another life-giving church is irrelevant. A win for the kingdom is a win for Healing Place Church.

Our heart is for people to encounter the hope and love of Jesus, but whether they come to our church or another life-giving church is irrelevant.

Just a few years before we started our church, there had been some less-than-positive situations in our community involving church leaders and Christian organizations. Many people had been hurt by their experience with church and had just walked away from everything to do with it. We figured a good place to start was simply to reach out and serve people, and if we were able to leave them with a good impression of Jesus and His church and to show them that we valued them, then it was worth it. Our goal was to turn them from the mindset that churches just take from people and leave them hurting to, "Wow, these people truly care about me and helped me with no strings attached; I want to know more about this kind of Jesus."

Outreach like this — just giving to people to show them you care — means investing finances into changing lives. There is a financial toll on the road of bringing healing to a hurting world. But I have been amazed over and over again whenever I look back at how faithful God has been to us. As we have invested our dollars to reach hurting people, He has always provided everything we needed. Whatever sacrifice we have made as a church He has more than repaid in the form of changed lives.

Now, more than fifteen years later, I am humbled by the opportunities God has given us to love and to serve countless people. I'm so happy we decided we would serve our community with His love and simply trust Him to bring in the people. It's like I mentioned earlier: if we are willing to take care of people outside the walls of our church, then He will take care of filling up the inside. And He has never let us down.

There's a cost to a servolution, but it's worth it.

IT OFTEN COSTS MORE THAN MONEY

It sure would be nice if everyone would just be happy about an organization focused on meeting the needs of the hurting and the oppressed—for people to celebrate the fact that someone is feeding the poor and helping the lost in the community. It definitely would make sense that fellow churches and Christian organizations would appreciate the work of another trying to shine a bright light for Jesus. Too bad it isn't always that way. It seems like there's always someone who is going to fight against what you're doing for the kingdom.

On the one hand, I know no one should go into ministry with the goal of being popular. We do what we do because we have a heart for Jesus and a desire to help people. And we don't always do everything perfectly. But on the other hand, criticism often comes for no good reason, and many times it comes from those within the Christian community. Criticism can be very powerful, and it takes only a few negative people to get the pastor's ear or drain energy from the vision of an organization.

When DeLynn and I launched this church, it was called Trinity Christian Center. It was a nice, safe, holy name. People could relate to it and assume what they were going to get. But it wasn't a clear reflection of who we were or what God had intended us to become. Sure, we believe in the Trinity, we operate on Christian principles, and we are at least somewhat centrally located. But we knew God had much more in store for us; so a few years later when God began dealing with me about a name change, I wasn't surprised. I do have to admit I wasn't too excited about the idea of rocking the status quo.

I asked a few key staff members what they thought about changing our name to the one I felt God wanted: Healing Place Church. Responses ranged from, "Trinity is a good name and we've earned a great reputation," and, "If it ain't broke, don't fix it," to, "It kinda sounds like a church that plays with snakes and sells diet pills," and, "When do we start serving organic high-fiber rice cakes?" After these reactions, I decided to hold up on the idea. But God, in His kind-but-firm way, reminded me this wasn't something He wanted anyone's input on. This was His idea and I had to choose between the advice of those around me and the instructions given by the God of the universe, the Creator of everything from nothing, the all-powerful, ever-loving God. When I thought about it that way, I knew what I had to do.

The next weekend at church, right before I began the message, I just did it. I stood on the stage and told everyone, "Hey, by the way, from now on we're going to be Healing Place Church, not Trinity Christian Center. Just thought you should know. Now turn in your Bibles to the book of Matthew." That was it. Sure, it was a little (okay, a lot) abrupt, but I *knew* it was what God wanted, and the time for discussion about it was long past.

I think God wanted to make sure we all understood that our mission is not only about helping the people who attend our services but also about reaching out and actually being a healing place for a hurting world. Why not allow our name to reflect our God-given identity? And to be honest, it didn't take long to help our church family embrace the concept.

Some of the other church leaders in our city, however, weren't so accepting. After the new name went up on the sign outside the church, I began to hear their disapproval of many of the ways we were reaching out to hurting people in our community. It was as though changing the name drew their fire against us for stuff we'd been doing all along anyway. "Are you seriously helping single moms?" "Wait ... you're marrying people in your church that aren't even Christians?" One pastor even came to me and said,

"Dino, you are lowering the standard for everybody. You are teaching compromise and cheapening grace."

That is not at all the way I see it. We simply decided to invite people to come freely to the one who paid the ultimate price for us. Jesus freely gave His grace to the woman caught in adultery and to so many others He encountered as He walked the earth. We just want to remove all the barriers between people and their opportunity to encounter the grace and love of Jesus. Whatever it takes.

Several years ago I was part of a pastors' meeting in our community. It became obvious very quickly that what we were doing at Healing Place Church simply did not fit into their concept of church. Louisiana is rich in religious tradition, and far too often the mindset of churches is that unsaved people should get cleaned up first, then come to church, and maybe we'll welcome them if they look enough like the rest of us. I guess the idea that churches would be a place that hurting people can come to find healing and hope — that hurting, dirty, needy people with problems would actually come inside of — was too scary of a thought for some of these guys to tolerate.

As I was sitting there hearing all of this, one of the pastors stood up and said, "Well, you know, there's a church in town now that's just *full* of sinners. I don't think there's a saved one in the bunch, and worse yet, the pastor doesn't even care that they're coming to the church." I thought, *Dude! I'm sitting right here!* I held my tongue, but I was honestly saddened that a church leader would see things this way. And as you can guess, we got plenty of backlash from this type of people for outfitting the kitchen at the Nation of Islam center. We were showing love to those who could be called our enemies, and as we did, we were catching flack from other churches.

This response was hard for DeLynn and me to deal with at first; we were doing something new, reaching out in a new way, taking risks that had not been taken in our city before, and the disapproval from our "peers" didn't make it easier. Still today, there are those in our community who disapprove of what we do, but we have learned not to worry about that and instead simply to stay busy with the task that God has given us.

I guess for DeLynn and me, the decision to serve whether it is popular or not, regardless of what it costs us, all goes back to one night about a year after we started the church.

IT ALL BELONGS TO GOD ANYWAY

It was 3:00 a.m. The obnoxious ring of the phone woke me up from dreamland. I gathered just enough consciousness to mutter, "Hello?"

"Preacher, your house is on fire!"

My brain went into full throttle. "What?" I frantically tried to wake DeLynn, telling her to get out of the apartment. "No, man!" the caller shouted through the phone. "Not the apartment you're in. It's the house you're building. It's burning down!"

I felt a momentary sense of relief. "Oh, whew. Wait ... no ... what?" Then my mind really started racing. We were nearly finished with construction on what would have been our first house.

A few minutes later I was watching as firefighters battled the blaze. The air smelled of burning wood, emergency lights flashed in the smoke, and I could hear the firefighters' chatter on their radios. Across the street, a crowd had gathered, neighbors in their pajamas wanting to see what all the commotion was about.

One of the firefighters came and stood by me. "Man ... I wonder whose house that was," he asked, still watching the unbelievable scene. The house wasn't going to make it and we both knew it.

"Uh ... that would be me," I told him, dazed. He looked at me for a couple of seconds then simply said, "Wow. Bummer." I thought to myself, *Make that "big bummer." As a matter of fact, this is even beyond "huge bummer."* And yet all I could do was stand there and stare, watching our dream of a new house go up in smoke.

As I stood there, a thought hit me. "So you want to help the poor and hurting, do you?" I knew the devil was well aware that our young church had been gaining more and more momentum in our servolution helping the poor and hurting.

I also knew he really would have loved to scare us away from our mission. "Are you really sure you want to help the poor and hurting? Because if you keep going, I'll burn down everything you have." I can still hear the devil's threat like it was yesterday.

A verse came to mind that gave me the encouragement I needed: "God anointed Jesus of Nazareth with the Holy Spirit and power, and ... he went around doing good and healing all who were under the power of the devil, because God was with him" (Acts 10:38).

The last part of the verse really jumped at me: "God was with him." And that's all I needed to know. I thought about that for a few more minutes as I watched the last of our house burn to the ground.

Then as the night sky began to break with a sunrise, I turned to go back to my car and said this simple prayer: "Jesus, everything I have is Yours, and that includes this house that just burned down. It is Yours, so I'll let You take care of this situation. I'm going home. There's more stuff I've got to do today to help some poor and hurting people."

It didn't seem like much at the moment, but I have looked back at that prayer as a defining moment. I knew this was my Boston Tea Party. I knew I had thrown a bunch of tea into the harbor that night and the revolution was on. DeLynn and I had decided to cross the line into servolution no matter what it cost us, and we have never regretted it.

Servolution will cost you. It will require finances, it will tax you emotionally, and it will drain you physically. And just when you think you've made it out of the woods, sometimes you'll be hit with a big ol' spiritual battle. However, the clock is ticking. We cannot simply spend our time making our lives more comfortable while so many around us are going to hell. As far as we are concerned at HPC, there is no price too high to deter us from our servolution. We will continue to be aggressive in our pursuit to show the love and grace of Jesus to as many people as possible before the clock runs out. And what a reward we will see when we get to heaven! It will be packed with people from our community whose lives have been transformed through this servolution.

SERVOLUTION STRATEGY

God showed me something one night when I woke up hungry and decided to sneak a bowl of cereal. I prowled into the kitchen at about 2:30 a.m., grabbed a box of Peanut Butter Crunch, and pulled out a big Tupperware bowl. I didn't use one of those little china dishes. No real man eats out of a glass bowl after two in the morning. You get some "big plastic" and pour about half a box of cereal and grab a big ol' serving spoon.

I stepped back for a second to survey the scene, and I was touched. A quiet but satisfied sigh escaped my lips. All I needed now was the milk, so I went to the fridge, opened the door, reached in, and found the gallon of vitamin D. As I pulled out the half-full carton, I noticed something that suddenly changed everything. The expiration date was a week old.

My heart was broken. But I'll never forget that night, not so much because of the heartbreak I felt over the milk but because of what happened next. As I tried to eat that huge Tupperware bowl full of dry Peanut Butter Crunch, I sensed the Holy Spirit saying to me, "Son, just like every gallon of milk has an expiration date, every single person has an expiration date. Every time you look into someone's eyes, remember that there is an expiration date on that person. The bad news is that they don't know the date. But the good news is that they don't have to expire alone. You need to tell them to get ready and to live ready."

Let me encourage you to set aside some time for self-reflection.

1. *Count the cost.* What are some of the sacrifices involved in beginning a servolution? How will serving others cost me personally?

2. *Reject fear.* When have I been criticized for reaching out to others? Are there outreaches God has laid on my heart to engage in, but I've hesitated because I feared criticism?

3. *Face your discouragement.* What are some of the discouragements I've faced while serving others? How do I usually respond to discouragement?

4. *Fanning the flames.* Have the people in my organization become complacent in regard to serving those less fortunate than themselves? If so, how can I rekindle their fire?

My friend Craig Groeschel[1] always reminds me that it all boils down to how much pain you're willing to go through for the cause. As ministry leaders, we can never allow ourselves to become apathetic to the fact every person has an expiration date. When you and I are in heaven, we will no longer have any more opportunities to help people choose Jesus. Let's make the most of our time on earth.

And I would say it is all worth it. All the sweat, resources, battles, opposition, and fatigue — they're *all worth it!* We must go rescue them.

CHAPTER 11

NO EXCUSES
165,000 EASTER EGGS

I believe it is vital for a church to do all it can to weave itself into the fabric of its community and to become part of the mosaic that makes up the region. A question I am always asking myself is, If HPC closed down tomorrow, who would notice? Would there be an outcry from the city for us to keep our doors open? If Healing Place Church disappeared from the map and no one felt the loss other than those who attended services, then we would have failed miserably.

Countless churches across the globe ranging from small assemblies to enormous congregations want to make a difference in the world and desire to have a positive influence in their communities. This is happening for many churches, and I believe it can happen for every one of them. It all starts by serving.

Healing Place Church has become an influential part of our region, a direct result of our ongoing servolution. Notice I used the word *ongoing*. Servolution has to be more than just a Healing Place for a Hurting World slogan or an exciting, energy-filled service or a blowout weekend outreach event. We do our best to do all of those things, but servolution is not just something that we do; it has become who we are. And the good news is that as long as we stay true to who we are — to what God has called us to be — we will never need to worry about having to close our doors.

Servolution is not just something that we do; it has become who we are.

At this point, some of you may be thinking a servolution is something that works great for us here at Healing Place Church in Baton Rouge, but that it couldn't work where you are. "Our people just don't have that kind of compassion," or, "We don't have the resources we'd need to pull off something like that," or (and I hear this one all the time), "We don't have any poor people in our community." If any of these thoughts have even remotely crossed your mind, then this section is for you. I'm going to unpack some of the strategic makings of a servolution and give you ideas for how to start from the beginning, how to expand what you may already be involved in, and how you can incorporate servolution into your culture.

THE STRATEGIC MAKINGS OF A SERVOLUTION

Excuse 1: Our church just doesn't have that kind of compassion.
Response: It starts with leadership—if you lead the way, the people will follow.

Servolution will not start in your church with a bunch of volunteers or even a few key leaders; it must begin within the heart of the pastor. When DeLynn and I started the church, we understood there was a reason God chose us to pastor in our city during this time. He had something specific for us to do, a particular way for us to serve, and a vision that He wanted us—as a church—to fulfill.

We know that ultimately we are going to have to give an account to God for what we do while we are on this planet, so from the beginning, we decided what was important to Him must be what we value the most: people. We decided we would serve people and leave the rest up to Him.

Servolution comes from the top down, or maybe it's more accurate to say from the inside out. All of our pastors and leaders lead with the message *and* the example of serving people "whatever, whenever." As you teach and train your staff, your leadership team, and your congregation about God's passion to reach out to the lost and the hurting, they will begin to develop the desire to serve as well. What's cool is that they may very well be able to see needs from a different angle than you could ever see on your own, and to come up with creative ways to meet those needs.

Regardless of where your church is, it's not an accident you are where you are, leading in your unique community. God has distinct purposes for your church, and He has already begun to put around you the kind of people required to fulfill that mission. As a leader, if you place before your congregation the vision of reaching the world by serving one, and the message of meeting the needs of the lost and the hurting, then this attitude and desire will spread throughout the culture of your church. It will ignite a servolution.

It is to the point now for us that when we are considering anything new, we always ask ourselves, How will this decision affect the poor and hurting? I had a guy come up to me once and say, "Pastor, I want to start a men's group that's not an outreach, but have it just be for some of us Christian guys to hang out together and bond." My response was, "I'm sorry, but we're never going to have something here at Healing Place Church that is only about us. That's not who we are."

For instance, our senior adult ministry can't just be about senior adults sitting around with the same friends every week talking about who won the '57 World Series.[1] While I have no problem with baseball and I don't mind having discussions about it, our small groups also need to be reaching out to the community. And our senior adults do. They are a vital part of our Cooking for Christ ministry, our greeters, our hospitality team, and numerous other outreaches. Our women's ministry does not spend all year meeting simply to catch up on what God has done for them and the latest in their family news; they regularly serve and give to the women in our community through events like Healing Place Women Pamper Nights[2] and helping out with a local shelter for battered women. Our women love serving. Our senior adults love serving. The same is true for our men, our students, even our children. Any way you cut us, we bleed servolution.

Any way you cut us, we bleed servolution.

Excuse 2:   We don't have the money to do outreach like that.
Response: Do what you can with what you have and see what God does.

We began with a small budget, and as the church increased in size, so did that budget. The time and energy we gave to community outreach in the beginning was small compared with the cumulative man-hours we serve on any given week today. But we were giving it all then just like we are now. The point is we started out doing what we could with what we had, and eventually, serving became how we do ministry and a huge factor in everything we do today.

Regardless of how much money you *don't* have, do what you can with what you do have. Serving will increase your capacity to change the world. Start with what you have, and watch what God does with it.

Excuse 3:   We just don't have any poor people in our community.
Response: Take another look.

In some regions, like here in Louisiana, poverty is relatively easy to find because our state has had such a long history of having a weak economy. The need is obvious. But just because the need isn't staring you in the face doesn't mean there are no poor and hurting people around you who need a servolution. Sometimes you just have to look a little harder, listen a little closer ... Are there people going through a divorce? Are there some who have lost their jobs? Are there people who are lonely with no family or friends? Are there widows, single moms, or people with special physical needs? Whether you're looking for them in a country club in Colorado or in Kenya's high-density slums at Kibera, there are always people nearby who are hurting or poor.

It may be natural to think you don't have any poor and hurting people in your community, but I guarantee you they are there. If there's an emergency room, there's someone hurting. If there's a funeral home, there's someone suffering a loss. Think about it for a minute. If there's a courthouse or jail, there's someone hurting. Someone once told me that since there were no poor people in their community, their outreach had to be pretty much limited to giving a check to their local food bank every month. I asked if they'd ever thought about going to see who was getting food from that food bank. Chances are, there's someone who's hurting, someone in need whom you can serve. We just often don't see them or know where to look. Take another look around you.

It's a good idea to ask God to open your eyes to help you see what might not be so obvious. It's true that some types of hurt and poverty are not easy to recognize. But I assure you, the poor and hurting are all around you. You just need to ask God to help you find them, and let Him show you how to serve them.

One of my friends is a pastor in another state, and he asked me to share in his church about our servolution. I told stories of some of the things we have experienced reaching people, cooking and giving to the poor, and handing out free water. I encouraged them to serve the poor and hurting in their community. Afterward, he told me how inspired and challenged they all felt, but that his region was very different from mine. Apparently, there are laws that restrict them from giving out food or from cooking in the open and offering free meals; plus, there were no financially poor people. (He wasn't just making excuses. In his area, there really isn't much of the level of poverty and unemployment we see all the time in my state.) My reply was, "Well, they may be harder to find, but there are still people here who need to be served. Sometimes a servolution requires a lot of creativity." He agreed, and his team went after it.

Not long after this meeting, he called me to tell me they had found a creative way to serve at a nearby prison. They needed tutors for the inmates, so they sent many qualified volunteers to serve in this area. They began to build relationships with these inmates and came up with an idea: "Let's adopt a hundred of these families for Christmas." What a servolution—to help hundreds of single moms, children, and parents at a time of year they could be hurting the most! This pastor was unwilling to let those needs go unmet. His attitude was, "We can't help everybody, and we can't do everything, but we can do something." And that heart is where servolution begins.

No matter where you are, there are hurting people in your community needing to be helped and served, people who need to be told they are not forgotten and are important to God. You could start by asking yourself and your leadership team what kinds of injustices are stirring your hearts and what types of burdens you are praying for. Many times you will find a starting point right there. Sometimes God will give you only a notion or a tug or a hunch about a particular outreach, but if you will be faithful to go out on a limb and share it with your congregation, you might be surprised at how quickly they embrace the vision.

A COUPLE OF WORDS OF ADVICE

1. START SMALL

Once you have committed in your hearts to begin a certain community outreach, start small before you go big. Trust me—it's so much easier to let something out of the can in a small environment where you can iron out the details that can make or break your outreach.

For example, one of our favorite outreaches is a water giveaway. As you can imagine, summers in Louisiana bring stifling heat and humidity. So we often give away thousands of bottles of water to people walking around in the city or sitting in traffic at intersections. The first few times we did it, we gave out only a few cases and we gave away Coke and Diet Coke. But because we started this outreach small, we were able to see some ways to improve, and we developed a few fundamentals of water giveaways.

First, the water needs to be iced down a certain amount of time before distributing it, and that amount changes depending on where you are giving it out. In some areas, the water can be dispersed quickly, but in others, it takes a lot longer, so the bottles need to be colder.

Second, when using coolers to transport dozens of bottles of water from trucks to the distribution point, coolers with wheels are a huge help.

Third, we switched to giving away water instead of Coke, not because of the evils of sugar and aspartame, and not even so much because of the lower cost of water, but just because of the wider acceptance that plain old ice-cold water has on the streets of Baton Rouge.

Fourth, we learned the value of including a small card with our church name, phone number, web address, and the following message on it: "We hope this small gift brightens your day. It is a simple way to say God loves you—no strings attached. Let us know if we can help you."

Simple details like this helped us to make our service excellent and our message clear, and helped to increase our capacity for this type of outreach.

2. DO A WALK-THROUGH FIRST

One time when we got a bit over our heads was with an Easter egg hunt. I will say, we did follow our own advice and started out small the first year. It was held on our church campus with about seventy to eighty kids, and the event was safe and smooth. The following year, we said, "Hey, let's do it again, but this time let's do it at the state fairgrounds!" We bumped everything up and planned for a bit of an increase, but nothing like what we saw the morning of the event. We were shocked when more than two thousand people arrived, baskets in hand, excited to join in on a massive egg hunt. We were undermanned, underprepared, and understocked. We hadn't planned for the outreach to grow from less than a hundred to more than two thousand in one year. Our team worked harder than ever and did the best we could and avoided a total train wreck. People were blessed and I'm sure many had a positive experience, but we knew it was far less than it could and should have been.

But we learned from our mistakes, and two years later offered our community an event we called The World's Largest Egg Hunt. We had 165,000 eggs on the ground, and when seven thousand people showed up, we were prepared. The event was a big win, and many people in our church today look back at that event as their first encounter with Healing Place Church.

Now we use this hard-learned lesson as a guide not only with new outreaches we start but also with the ones we realize are about to grow exponentially. This is the lesson: as a team, we need to place ourselves in the event long before it begins. Envisioning it helps to determine how it will actually work and what won't work. From there we are able make adjustments beforehand, rather than on-the-fly during the event.

> **As a team, we need to place ourselves in the event long before it begins. Envisioning it helps to determine how it will actually work and what won't work.**

Remember as you read our testimony of the Healing Place Church servolution, it has been more than sixteen years in the making. Some of the outreaches and ministries we offer today we never could have imagined just five or ten years ago. It didn't happen overnight. We definitely have made our share of mistakes and still don't have all of the answers. We are still learning on this journey of servolution.

Our entire staff, leadership team, and congregation have grown with each new year and with each new experience along the way. Our level of compassion and capacity to respond have increased, and our awareness of the needs around us has been sharpened. This is because we have chosen to put a high value on investing our time, effort, resources, and attention to serving people and meeting their needs. It has been a process and a great deal of hard work, but I assure you, every moment of it has been worth the cost.

Servolution simply cannot happen without resulting in a stronger, healthier, more fulfilled church. The sense of being a part of making a real difference in the world will bring life to the people in your church in ways you cannot imagine.

SERVOLUTION STRATEGY

What makes an outreach worthwhile in the kingdom does not depend on whether it is a new idea. It isn't a contest to see who can do the craziest outreach. What is important is how outrageous the love is that is shown in the outreach. Here's how to make sure yours is top-notch.

We try to make every event as warm and welcoming as possible. One way we do this is to go through the event as clearly as possible before the event takes place. We have people on our team whose job it is to act like a visitor, and they ask these questions:

- I've never been to Healing Place Church before, and I'm walking in ... Do I need instructions?
- Do I know what's going on?
- Are the people friendly? Do I feel like an outsider?
- Do I feel like I'm second rate? Am I embarrassed about my need or about how I'm dressed?

By walking through this process, we are able to test ourselves, to work through otherwise unforeseeable issues, discover the people who have a heart for the particular areas of service for that outreach, and plan properly for the event before it actually starts.

1. *Visitor-friendly events.* What questions do you ask to ensure that your events are friendly and welcoming to visitors and guests?

2. *Walk it through.* What process have you developed to "walk-through" your events before they happen?

3. *Start small.* What is an example of a way you can get started this week with a "small" idea? (See appendix 1 for ideas.)

CHAPTER 12

SERVOLUTION STREET

THE NEIGHBORHOOD WHERE JESUS LIVES

People thrive when they are fighting side by side for a common cause. It's human nature. If you ever want to see the crowd mentality up close and personal, just come down to an LSU football game. You'll see more purple and gold on more screaming people than you ever thought possible, and before you know it, you'll be yelling your head off, "Geaux Tigers!" just like the rest of them. There's a powerful and tangible energy present when people come together, united with a shared mission, and work passionately side by side to accomplish any task. (Even if it's just to cheer their team on to win yet *another* LSU championship ... but who's counting?) This shared experience leaves a lasting impression on every single participant; they are now connected to each other by the memory of the time and effort they invested and the incredible energy they experienced. A contagious spirit like that can spread like a virus through a church congregation. The result is a stronger and more unified body.

A perfect example of this happened several weeks after Hurricane Katrina. Our country has seen many natural disasters, but rarely has a disaster happened in such a densely populated metropolis as New Orleans is. Millions of people were affected by the devastation of this event, and even today — years later — there is still much to be done. Because of the flooding, hundreds of churches were destroyed, but fortunately, some were able to be restored, like the Franklin Avenue Baptist Church.

It was a typical ninety-degree day, and we joined more than five hundred other volunteers who had descended on the site ready to work. Because the church had soaked in fifteen feet of filthy water for several hot days, the entire building needed to be gutted.

Everyone who was assigned to work inside the building was required to cover every inch of their bodies with protective gear: rubber gloves, coveralls, boots, hats, goggles, and breathing apparatuses. We looked like we were ready for a walk on the moon. In addition, we were told that what we'd be breathing while working inside the church could be toxic. No one hesitated for even a moment. We walked right in and began working.

People were working in unbearable conditions and yet when they came out to change shifts, they looked like an offensive line coming off the field after a long drive for a touchdown — dirty and exhausted, but loving every moment of the grueling servolution and feeling so privileged simply to have the opportunity to participate in the team effort, thriving together for a common cause.

RATS!

Another extreme example of the strengthening effects of a servolution took place in the early days of our dream center in Donaldsonville, Louisiana. We had acquired a property with a building on it that had previously been a beer warehouse and then a potato chip factory. We were told the building should be condemned, but we also knew God had other plans. Our team went to work clearing out the old, run-down brick warehouse, which had been out of commission for years. There were leftovers — broken palettes, trash, scraps of junk, piles of garbage, and whatever else the previous occupants decided they didn't want to clean up.

It stank. It was filthy. It looked at first like an overwhelming job. And that's when the rats decided to come out from hiding. Not one or two. Not a dozen or two. No, it was dozens and dozens—easily over a hundred of them. Derek Smith was one of the warriors that day and recalled the battle that ensued: "We grabbed hoes, pitchforks, and shovels—whatever we could find—and went in there swinging. Rats were everywhere. It was like every time we'd swing, we'd kill something." By the time the battle was over, Derek and the crew had made a pile of dead rats about four feet high in the parking lot outside. They cleaned, cleared out rubble, cleaned again, renovated, and cleaned some more, and now that formerly rat-infested building is a key part of our dream center training facility and church campus.

It stank. It was filthy. It looked at first like an overwhelming job. And that's when the rats decided to come out from hiding.

Here's the point—the guys that went through that rat battle together now hold a special bond with each other that can come only from standing back to back fending off oversized rodents in a dark, dingy, humid, abandoned warehouse—for the cause of Christ. Serving together builds internal strength in our relationships.

IDENTIFY THE "SERVE"

By serving together over the years, our church family has matured together, deepened friendships with each other, and grown spiritually in Christ. Introducing servolution into your church—or taking it to the next level—is one of the best strategies to help your people realize their value and find more fulfillment as they learn to serve with new gifts and talents.

As leaders, we can help people identify their "serve." It's that ache in their hearts that compels them to respond to certain needs.

Many times, it is related to their own experiences, but sometimes, it's just a God-given compassion for a specific need. For instance, while an outreach for drug addicts moves one person because his father was an alcoholic who abused his mother, another person might not be moved as much by this need; *he* is moved by the need to help AIDS orphans in Africa. While one woman has a heart to help elderly people because she had wonderful relationships with her grandparents, another has little context for that need but spends her time teaching children with special needs. In every person's heart resides a cause, and when we help people identify what compels them to serve, we are well on our way to a full-on servolution.

The truth is every person in your congregation has a serve. Yes, even the woman who has been coming for a decade and never talks. Yes, even the guy who — on a good day — looks like he'd slap his grandma just to get the last piece of pecan pie. There is a place for everyone. Sure, some people may think they would rather just come to church each week and never get involved. But as you consistently communicate the servolution vision and empower people to serve, you'll be surprised by how many come ready to do whatever, whenever. Here are some of the things we talk about on a regular basis to keep building servolution momentum.

1. You have something to offer. I think a lot of people go to bed at night thinking they don't have anything significant to offer. They have a sincere desire to take part and to serve, but they think someone else could do it better, or they are afraid they might put themselves out there and fail. As church leaders we need to guard against a mindset that is so consumed with the cause that we forget those whom God has given to us as partners in this servolution.

Here in Louisiana, gumbo is one of many incredible foods we enjoy. There are about as many ways to make gumbo as there are Cajuns. But one thing is key to a good gumbo: lots of ingredients.

You can put just about anything in a gumbo—andouille,[1] shrimp, chicken, okra, crab claws, oysters, and even boiled eggs and some onion tops.[2] And just like a good gumbo, it seems the more you put into a servolution, the better it gets.

We speak regularly in our services about every person having their own God-given gifts that are useful ingredients in the servolution gumbo. All ages, all personality types, and all cultures can share the love of Christ with a person in need, and however they express Christ, our servolution needs it!

They also need to be assured that when they come to serve, they will be valued and loved and taught exactly what they need to know to succeed. If a volunteer shows up and nobody welcomes them but just assigns them to a post with no guidance, they aren't going to feel valued. Even worse, if they show up and the leaders are too busy to notice them and to help them get involved, then they will walk away feeling invisible. Strive to make serving fun, to celebrate wins, and to load volunteers up with a ton of gratitude. When you do this, people will know that they are part of the team and that what they personally added to the gumbo pot was significant.

2. Serving is the best way out of your pain. There are so many people in church congregations who are new in Christ or who are in the middle of a crisis or tragic loss or who are walking through tremendous needs of their own. Healing Place Church is no exception; remember, our mission statement is to be a healing place for a hurting world. People come here and say, "I am hurting so badly. Can you help stop the aching?" One of the most important things we tell them is, "You need to get involved with serving someone else's need. As you serve, watch what God does to your need."

We try to help people understand that sometimes the best way out of our hurt is when we choose to look outside ourselves to notice another person's pain. One of the surest ways to have a revolution in our own lives is when we begin to serve others.

Suddenly our situations, our pains, our struggles, and our disappointments don't seem as bad. There's a natural painkiller that comes as our focus is diverted from our own struggles to becoming part of the healing of another's pain. Often when we come back to our issue, we discover that a healing has occurred. Our wound isn't as deep; the scar isn't as noticeable as before.

I have watched a tremendous example of this in a young lady in our church.[3] While Natalie was attending LSU, her mother and father both passed away. In separate incidents, they suffered fatal brain aneurisms — within months of one another. Natalie was devastated; she felt like her life was over. But rather than give in to those feelings, Natalie embedded herself deeply in serving others. She enrolled in our Healing Place School of Ministry[4] internship, studying ministry and serving alongside our staff for two years. All the while, she was still working through her own loss.

As part of her internship, Natalie went to Africa on two short-term missions to serve with Children's Cup, caring for children who have been abused, neglected, and even abandoned. She experienced an instant connection with these precious little kids, many of whom had lost their parents to AIDS. Even though her life story was different, Natalie could identify with the orphans' loss.

Out of her own pain, she served, loved, hugged, and played games with the children. Just a few months after graduating from HPSM, she went back to Africa to serve a one-year term with Go Global,[5] helping to launch the new Healing Place Church campus in Swaziland. Part of her role at this time was to serve at the care points, ministering to the AIDS orphans she loves.

By serving her way through her pain, Natalie has taken an experience that could have destroyed her life and allowed God to turn it into something significant for the children of Swaziland. What an amazing journey of healing!

3. There is a place for you to fit in. Our volunteers need to trust that we will fit them where they can serve best. Some people do well talking with other people about their faith or leading worship in front of the church. Others might feel like their hearts would explode from pounding in fear if they had to serve that way. There are hundreds of ways people can serve others without ever having to stand in front of an audience. They can set up chairs, hand out balloons, paint faces, repair bikes, grill hotdogs, and smile and give kids cotton candy. When you break it down to the basics, just about everyone can do one of those things. We try to create a variety of opportunities so people with different personalities and interests can have a role in the servolution. Now, everyone gets to be a part of the harvest.

We also invest a significant amount of time and energy getting to know our volunteers so that our leaders can steer them in the right direction. Some people are silk, and some people are sandpaper. We try not to have our sandpaper types at the entrance of the event welcoming guests and visitors. If we are going to serve our community, we need the silky types there greeting them and making a first impression that helps them to feel comfortable and accepted. On the other hand, we don't need a lot of silk on the team that's digging a ditch for a water line at our campus in Mozambique, or packing an ocean container with hospital gear headed for Honduras. That's where we need some "rough and tough" help. As leaders, we must speak about the importance of all types of gifts, recognize the gifts that people have, and then place our volunteers accordingly. We need all kinds of people to accomplish a multifaceted servolution.

People want to participate; people *need* to participate. When we, as leaders, give people opportunities to move beyond being spectators and into roles in which they can touch the needs of the hurting people in their communities, we will see them thrive like never before. They will experience a profound sense of personal value, fulfillment, and purpose. Their roots will grow deeper into the house of God, their relationships with Jesus and each other will mature, they will move from a place of hurt to a place of wholeness, and they will want to serve more and more.

Here is an account from one of our faithful volunteers that communicates the profound effect a servolution has on both the one being served and the one doing the serving:

I had the opportunity today to meet the people in my neighborhood, or more precisely, in the Baton Rouge Dream Center neighborhood. (I like to think of that as my neighborhood.) A few of us were downtown working at the warehouse, sorting boxes and pulling groceries. I was looking at some paperwork when Barbara came in and told me there was a man there that needed to talk to me. I went outside to find two men waiting by the door. I introduced myself, shook their hands, and asked how we could help them. The first gentleman told me that he had just gotten out of work-release (final phase of prison term) and was staying with a friend. He had a job lined up and money that was coming to him, but for right now he was hungry. He said someone had told him that we were a church that helped people. He wondered if we would help him. I smiled and nodded. I asked his friend if he could use some groceries too. He nodded and said it would be appreciated. I asked the volunteers to make a couple of boxes for the men. Then we gathered together and I asked how we could pray for them.

The first guy asked for prayer that the job he has lined up would come through. When I asked the second man how we could pray for him, he said, "I buried my wife on Sunday. She died on Mother's Day, but it took us some time to get things together for the funeral. My daughter is in Baton Rouge General. She has sickle cell disease and cysts on both ovaries, but praise God, she's being released today." It was all I could do not to weep. We joined hands and prayed for these precious souls. Before they left, I asked them about salvation ... not in so many words, but I had to know. Both assured me that they knew God. I told them that I never want to feed somebody's body and let them go to hell. They smiled and nodded, thanking us again for the groceries. They both plan on coming to the dream center tomorrow to volunteer.

A short while later a man came up, pushing a woman in a wheelchair. They too had heard that we sometimes help people. The woman had just gotten out of the hospital and had prescriptions that needed to be filled. I referred her to some local agencies that help with that and asked if they needed food. They said they had been homeless but recently found a place to live. As the volunteers made another food box, I told the woman about our support group on Friday mornings. She said she would come for sure. We all gathered together again and asked how we could pray for them. The woman needed healing in her leg and for things to get better. The man also needed healing, as last month he was shot by a security guard while on "the boat." We prayed for them and invited them back again tomorrow. Again, they both planned to come.

So, these are the people in my neighborhood: grieving widows, ex-prisoners, the lame, and the walking wounded. I believe this is the exact neighborhood where Jesus would choose to live. I'm so grateful that Healing Place Church allows us to serve this community. All glory to God!

SERVOLUTION STRATEGY

Here are some practical ideas for developing your ongoing servolution.

1. Train all your key leaders who work with volunteers to value people by
   - greeting *each one* with a warm welcome.
   - acknowledging their sacrifice of time and energy to serve.
   - never wasting a volunteer's time. Make sure every rehearsal, service opportunity, and outreach is carefully planned and organized.
   - thanking every volunteer before they leave and complimenting them on their specific contribution.
2. At least once a year, sponsor a great volunteer appreciation night, complete with food, games, and prizes.
3. Every now and then, take a few minutes during the service to communicate to the congregation a volunteer's testimony about a particular outreach.
4. Regularly ask your key leaders and volunteers about their thoughts on improvements and for new outreach ideas.

Take some time to reflect on the lessons of this chapter and discuss the following questions.

1. *Serving together.* How have you experienced the joy of serving together with other people? What happens when people serve together side by side?

2. *My serve.* What particular injustices in the world pull on your heart? What needs cause your heart to ache? What would you identify as your "serve"?

3. *The people in my neighborhood.* Who are the people in your neighborhood whom God has placed in your life for you to serve?

CHAPTER 13

KEEP YOUR SERVE ALIVE
AVOIDING COMPASSION FATIGUE

"Not called!" did you say? "Not heard the call," I think you should say.

Put your ear down to the Bible, and hear Him bid you go and pull sinners out of the fire of sin. Put your ear down to the burdened, agonized heart of humanity, and listen to its pitiful wail for help. Go stand by the gates of hell, and hear the damned entreat you to go to their father's house and bid their brothers and sisters and servants and masters not to come there.

Then look Christ in the face — whose mercy you have professed to obey — and tell Him whether you will join heart and soul and body and circumstances in the march to publish His mercy to the world.

— William Booth, founder of the Salvation Army

How in the world are we going to be able to keep doing this?
I was so surprised at that thought; I turned around to see if maybe I had heard it from someone else on the airplane. Nope. It must have been me, because there it was again: *How can I possibly keep up like this?*

For the past three weeks, I had been on the road: London, Washington, D.C., and Italy, and I was now just a few hours from landing in Baton Rouge. I was looking over my schedule for the next few weeks, trying to get mentally shifted for the tasks awaiting me at Healing Place Church, when the thought crossed my mind. *There's no way I can keep this up.*

I have to say, it's not as if I've never had thoughts like this. Anyone who takes a headfirst plunge into God's destiny for their life will probably have similar thoughts. Maybe you are feeling the same way right now. Although you've been inspired by the concept of servolution, you're already worn down and cannot imagine taking on a challenge like this.

I know how it feels to be "served out." I'm familiar with the temptation to settle into a more comfortable life in which there is no one else to serve — just me, myself, and I. But in my heart, I also know I would never be the least bit happy or satisfied living that way. So I've allowed God to teach me some ways that have helped me battle fatigue and keep my serve alive. I try to keep these concepts in front of our staff and congregation, because while we may be "A Healing Place for a Hurting World," none of us are immune to wearing out.

REMEMBER THE GRACE AND MERCY GOD HAS SHOWN YOU

In those times when I've worn down and have begun to focus on my tiredness, or when my desire to back off from things is stronger than my need to serve people, I remind myself of all that God has done in my life. I think about the grace and mercy Christ has given me, the ten thousand second chances He has offered me, how much He has forgiven me, and all that He has blessed me with. I don't just gloss over these things like I'm checking off a grocery list; I really think and meditate on how amazing God has been in my life. He's blessed me with an incredible wife and three healthy, beautiful children, and he's offered us the tremendous privilege to pastor a congregation filled with the most ridiculously cool people I have ever met. I mean that wholeheartedly!

After spending valuable time with these thoughts, how can I do anything other than to serve as many people as possible with my life? I become motivated by something higher; I'm inspired by the responsibility of the grace He has given me. It's like an alarm goes off in my heart, saying, "Come on, Dino. It's time to get up and help someone else find what you've found." Yes, I can choose to hit the snooze button and ignore the alarm, burying my head under a pillow of self-pity because I don't feel like getting up to serve. But when I remember what He's done for me, I find that God just won't let me sleep through this life.

Jesus tells a story about a servant who owed an incredible debt to his king.[1] When he could not pay the debt, the king ordered the man's family and possessions to be sold. The man fell at the king's feet, begging for mercy, and the king took pity on him and forgave his debt. The very next day that same servant found a man who owed *him* a tiny debt, and he became angry when the man could not pay. The man who owed the small debt fell at the servant's feet and pleaded, but the servant (who had just been completely forgiven by the king) showed him no mercy. He threw him in jail until he could pay his debt.

When the king found out about this injustice, he went to his servant and said, "You wicked servant! After I forgave your debt, you went out and snatched someone who owed you pennies and threw him in jail. So now I'm going to release that man, throw *you* in jail, and you will be tortured for doing this." The first dude forgot the grace and mercy he'd been shown, and as a result, he treated other people badly. I'm guessing he regretted that at this point.

The principle of this story is clear: forgotten grace and taken-for-granted mercy create a calloused heart. I never want to be like this. I want to operate out of a daily awareness of God's grace in my life. I want always to remember that I've been released from a debt I could never pay; I've been forgiven my many failures. I need to have God's grace alive in my heart today, and when I remind myself of all of this, I discover fresh motivation to serve the person next to me with an attitude that says, "I'll do whatever it takes, whenever it is needed."

Forgotten grace and taken-for-granted mercy create a calloused heart. I never want to be like this.

REMEMBER TO ENJOY THE JOURNEY

You can get to a point where all the aforementioned thoughts are about as effective as sucking on cotton when you're thirsty. They're all true, and you know they should turn up the compassion in your heart, but you're just too exhausted. You've hit a wall some call compassion fatigue. It is a condition resulting from being so busy serving people you begin to grow weary and become numb to the pain of those you're serving.

In our excitement to reach as many people as possible, we risk forgetting that each one of them is an individual. Each of them matters to God, and each has feelings; they hurt, they cry, and they have hopes and expectations—just like all of us do.

Compassion fatigue is the kind of problem that sneaks up on you in times when a need is overwhelming and the response requires a continual investment of large amounts of energy. And when you add the emotional toll this type of need can take, it can be easy to lose sight of the value of the individual.

Not surprisingly, we experienced compassion fatigue on a large scale a few months after Hurricane Katrina tore through Louisiana. As an entire church, we threw ourselves headlong at the need, giving everything we could in a hundred different ways.

After about four months of an extremely intense level of serving, it seemed as though everyone was exhausted, and there was still an overwhelming amount of work to be done.

So we decided to make a point of encouraging each other to remember the joy. I taught several weekends at church about living a joyful life and how to enjoy the abundant life God has provided for every one of us. We talked about who we are in Christ, and the importance of finding our identity in Him, not in our servolution. We discovered the refreshment of putting ourselves and our servolution in God's hands and allowing Him to renew our spirits, souls, and bodies.

REMEMBER TO TAKE GOOD CARE OF THE SERVOLUTIONARIES

Pastor John Osteen gave me some great advice on how to handle the finances of our church.

1. Pay your bills as soon as you get them.
2. Save a little money each month so you don't have to be constantly living from the bottom of the barrel. If you are always living off the bottom, and as a church you have no margin, you cannot be an effective resource to bless someone else.
3. Give to the poor, and support missions.
4. Give back to your people. Give back to those who work so hard to give to the church, and be a blessing to those who bless you.

At Healing Place Church, we have wholeheartedly followed his advice, especially in that fourth point. We do a lot of things simply to show our volunteers that we value them, love them, and want to bless them for all the time, effort, and finances they invest to help build the kingdom of God. Some Sundays, we give away Dippin' Dots for everyone, or on a Wednesday night, we give them a free CD of a recent service. Being in a culture that enjoys food passionately, we do a lot of eating as a church. There's just something about eating together that makes us want to stick around and be together. Whether it is a big crawfish boil for the band and choir, or a barbeque with the parking crew, or just a bunch of yard-bird[2] for everyone after a service, we continually look for ways to invest back into people and let them know they are appreciated.

We do a lot of eating as a church. There's just something about eating together that makes us want to stick around and be together.

One of the large thank-yous we give our people is some type of huge outdoor party during the spring or fall. We always have free food and drinks, and sometimes sno-cones or cotton candy, and as many of the biggest inflatable games as we can find. A couple of times, we did a massive fireworks display, and one time we even had hot air balloons all over the place — that was really cool to see. For a few years, we did these types of events at the state fairgrounds, but now we have the space to do them on our own property. We make it a point to let the church know they can bring friends and family and anyone else they might want to invite. We make it all free to anyone who comes — our way of thanking our people with a great event they can enjoy, and at the same time giving them an easy way to connect their friends and family with HPC as well. Sure, it costs a whole lot of money and energy to make an event like this come together, but it is stuff like this that lets people know we appreciate them.

As pastors, DeLynn and I are so grateful for the people of excellence God has provided to run every aspect of Healing Place Church, and we love to find opportunities to communicate this through blessing them. A couple of times we have gathered for a staff meeting (about a hundred of us) and given everyone an envelope with money in it (sometimes it's ten dollars, and sometimes a hundred). Then we tell everyone to meet at the mall simply so we all can spend some time together shopping. We love to give gifts to the staff. We also love to bring gifted speakers in for staff development and enrichment. And there's nothing like telling everyone to go home early or take the next day off. Especially around major events, it is very important that the staff be prepared *and* well rested so everyone can come in with their best. It's no good for the people we are serving if our staff greets them with furrowed brows and tired faces or are so intense about the task of helping them, they don't actually connect with anyone.

As a staff, we frequently talk about how to love and serve each other; if we can't succeed in serving here, then we're not going to be good at it outside our walls. We try to create opportunities for us all to be together and to have fun by hanging out together. Strong relationships throughout the team are a vital part of maintaining a healthy staff. When we, as a team, believe in each other and value each other, we are able to create some very effective environments for outreach. Also, it's amazing how many more volunteers will show up to serve when they know they will get to be a part of a team that is enjoying life.

So how can we keep doing this? It's a perfectly normal question to ask. As pastors who have chosen to give our lives to the service of others, and like every servolutionary, it is all too easy to allow ourselves to become tired and numb to the very heart we have dedicated our lives to. We need to remind ourselves of the great grace and mercy provided to us through Jesus, take the time to refresh ourselves, and show our appreciation for those who serve with us. Doing these things will help us to keep our edge, continue to be filled with the love and compassion Christ has for us, and turn that into fuel to ignite the next level of our servolution.

SERVOLUTION STRATEGY

It is important for every leader in ministry to take a few moments from time to time to assess fatigue and stress levels. If we allow ourselves to become too consumed by the "work" of the ministry, then we will not be effective when we are trying to minister to God's people.

1. *Rest and refreshment.* Have I been taking the appropriate time to refresh myself in God?

2. *Finding balance.* Have I been able to spend quality time with my family? With friends? Are the staff leaders and key volunteers feeling overwhelmed? If so, how can we help to make them feel balanced in their use of time and to feel appreciated? As a leader, am I asking the right questions to gain understanding about how my staff or volunteers are doing? Do they feel the freedom to admit when they might need to take a rest?

3. *Celebration and thanksgiving.* When was the last time I called the staff or volunteers into a meeting just for the purpose of thanking them for all their efforts? When was the last time the church blessed them with a gift?

CHAPTER 14

NEVER
SERVE ALONE
WHERE'S MY HIGH FIVE?

I was on top of the world. Healing Place Church was only a few years old, and we were busting out of the walls. The church was growing like crazy, and we were out of space in our services every weekend. We had added a Saturday night service, and we still needed more room. My mind was racing through what it all meant and where it was headed. I was sitting at my gate in the Baton Rouge Metropolitan Airport waiting to board a flight for a speaking engagement in Minnesota.

God was blessing everything we were doing, and I had just come through a weekend of phenomenal church services. I sat back and closed my eyes, and my imagination took off to Mount Everest. I saw myself standing on the peak of the world's tallest mountain, fully geared up with a forty-pound expedition backpack, goggles, boots, helmet, and mountain axe. Snow whirled around me as gusts of winds fought against my rugged silhouette. I, Dino Rizzo, had conquered the mountain. I wanted to celebrate, to give someone a high five, and that was when I realized something was missing.

I was all by myself. There was nobody there — nobody to hug, nobody to chest-butt, nobody to share the moment with. If I wanted to post a picture of this on my blog, I was going to have to aim the camera back at myself and take the shot of me standing there alone.

I sat up from the daydream and thought, *What a sad picture.*

Sitting on the plane that Sunday afternoon, I made a decision: we are not going to experience mountaintops alone. We are going to share these experiences with other people, and when we climb to summits, we're going to have people up there with us to celebrate the victories and to enjoy the views. And in those times when the path we choose doesn't actually get us to a summit, those friends will be there to help us through the defeats. From that realization, DeLynn and I determined to become proactive about making solid, intimate relationships with other people. We wanted to share this journey of leading a church and doing life with as many quality friends as possible. As a result, a focus on growing strong, healthy relationships became an important value in the culture of our church as well.

I wanted to celebrate, to give someone a high five, and that was when I realized something was missing.

It's a biblical model, really. When Jesus called many of the twelve disciples, he sought those who had established relationships with one another. For instance, Matthew tells the story of Jesus' calling two brothers, Simon Peter and Andrew, as they worked on their fishing boats.[1] Jesus called them to come and follow Him into the ministry, and immediately they both dropped what they were doing to be a part of what He was doing. Then Jesus saw two other brothers, James and John, cleaning their fishing nets, and He invited them to join Him as well. Both brothers left their family's fishing business to join Jesus' ministry. In fact, before following Jesus, many of the twelve disciples had some prior connection to each other, through family, a business relationship, or living in the same neighborhood.

I find all of this very interesting. I used to wonder why Jesus didn't pick twelve individuals from twelve different backgrounds and twelve different regions. Wouldn't the extra variety have been better in the long run? I now believe that Jesus carefully chose these men with previous connections and prior relationships because He knew what He was calling them into. He knew the servolution ahead of them would be filled with hardships, tremendous fear, persecution, and for most of them, martyrdom. He knew these men were going to need solid, committed friendships to be able to go through it all. Dealing with the arguments and jealousies that are common in these types of relationships would still be a whole lot simpler than trying to work with twelve, independent-minded loners. The fact that they were in relationship with each other gave them a head start for the task ahead.

It's the same way for you and me. We want to accomplish all the plans God has for us. We want to have the capacity to serve the multitudes of people He will bring us *and* not give up when it gets difficult along the way. I believe it will be much easier to do this if we are intentional in our relationships. Almost every single outreach we are involved in today was birthed out of a God-ordained relationship. I cannot overstress how integral this factor has been in the growth of our church and our servolution. Here are several of the insights I have gained throughout these years of developing intimate and committed friends.

NEVER SURF ALONE

I used to be an avid surfer, and during those younger years, my little Italian momma had only one rule about being in the water. Unlike most other moms' rule, it had nothing to do with a mandatory waiting period after eating my lunch. My momma's one rule was, "Never surf alone." No matter what the weather was like, no matter what the time was (even if it was four o'clock in the morning), I was allowed to go surfing as long as I had someone surfing with me. Looking back, I'm glad she laid down the law with that one, because there were times I took some foolish risks. In those situations, it was a good thing I had a partner around to bail me out when I sucked in too much water. Momma's rule saved my life on more than one occasion in the waters off Myrtle Beach, South Carolina. Now that I think of it, it has probably saved my life in ministry several times as well!

Too many of us in ministry want to surf alone. Often, we're either too busy with the work at hand to develop the friendships we need, or we're unwilling to share our doubts and fears with someone else. There's always a bunch of excuses we make up to convince ourselves that it's okay to hit the waves alone. Instead, we all need to take a serious look at how we are doing in our relationships. If we decide to go surfing in ministry without strong, healthy relationships in our lives, one day we'll find ourselves overwhelmed by the power of unexpected waves and the ever-changing currents of life.

INTERNAL DISORIENTATION

More than once when I was surfing, I crashed inside a huge wave. I spun out of control under the power of strong water currents. I became disoriented and could not tell which way was up. I tried to kick my legs downward to touch the ocean floor, hoping to spring myself back up to the surface. But I found that there was nothing there—just more water. My heart raced even faster at this point. I swam frantically toward the surface only to feel my head skimming along the sand at the bottom instead. Finding myself upside down, the instinct to panic was very strong. But then, in the midst of my fear, a hand reached toward me; it was my partner offering help, showing me what I couldn't see on my own—the way to the surface.

All of us who are involved in ministry eventually have moments when we don't have a clue where we are heading or how we are going to get where we're going or how we are going to pay for something. Many times I have asked myself or said to DeLynn, "What in the world are we doing?" I've had questions about handling a crisis a family is going through, about how to know when to make a change in the leadership of a ministry, or about how to pay for a new facility. We've all been there, dealing with disorientation.

All of us who are involved in ministry eventually have moments when we don't have a clue where we are heading or how we are going to get where we're going or how we are going to pay for something.

Strong relationships are vital because they can help us work our way through these times of disorientation. We can sit down with close friends or with mentors in the ministry to share our fears and insecurities and not be afraid that they are going to freak out. Sometimes, just knowing they are there to help bail you out if something goes wrong can give you the guts to do what you know you should do. Having friends around you can reduce the risk you face when launching new ministries or doing something new.

I'm not talking about the kind of friendships where you get together just to talk about the *highlights* of your ministries and how wonderfully successful every part of them is. I'm talking about the people you spend time with and in a matter of ten minutes you're unloading your *lowlights*. You're telling how you messed up the illustrated message last night by using a three wood to drive a plastic golf ball into the forehead of a little old lady who was sitting innocently in the tenth row, and how the guy behind her has decided to sue the church for psychological damage. You're also listening to your friends tell their stories of their troubles. But you're encouraging each other too, helping each other to see that none of you are alone in your struggles.

I want people in my life who will talk to me like this, unafraid to share their doubts and their fears, because if they can share with me how they got through their dark nights, then I will be encouraged to get through mine. I have never pastored a church before Healing Place Church. I haven't led a staff of a hundred before this. Because I've never done this before, it helps to have people around me who are walking through it too. I'm even blessed with some friends who have already been where I am, who help me navigate my journey. If you don't have people like this in your life, ask God to show you who He wants you to connect with in this way. He is the master of your destiny; He knows who needs to be in your life to help take you to the next destination, and who needs *you* to help them to theirs.

YOU MAY BE GOOD, BUT YOU'RE NOT THAT GOOD

When you surf, there's almost always the question of sharks. As one surfer, you can't possibly see everything going on around you, particularly under the surface. The more surfers there are out there with you, the greater the chance that someone will notice if a shark is in the area. In ministry, we all have blind spots, and sometimes only the people around us can identify when the danger in one is about to bite our leg off. There are so many ways for us to get distracted, so much garbage that can jam up our lives, and so much temptation just waiting to latch onto our hearts. But a close friend can save us from the sin, or simply even a misconception, that could take a huge bite out of our lives and ministries.

We all deal with pride and ego, but close relationships will help us keep them under control. I have friends who have earned the right to ask the hard questions like, "Okay, what's really going on?" and, "Why are you acting like that? Do you really think you're *that* good? Because you're not." They say it in a way that isn't mean — just a good reality check for me when I need it. Pride and ego will always try to come alive inside our hearts. But because of the depth of our relationship, a well-developed trust gives us the willingness to allow each other to scrape off those edges and keep us humble.

Some churches and organizations have a culture that if you're a pastor or leader and you're fighting something in your life, you need to keep it to yourself. It's like an antiperspirant commercial:

"Never let 'em see you sweat." Don't let on that you're not perfect. Just try to sort it out between you and God and hope in the meantime nobody notices that you don't know what you're doing. Just fast and pray—as long as it takes—until you get the answer. This isn't the strategy the Bible teaches. Throughout the New Testament are instructions for us to confess our faults to one another,[2] to encourage one another,[3] to carry one another's burdens.[4] None of us are good enough to discover all the answers by ourselves; we all need each other to find our paths through the jungle of life.

I have no problem calling one of my friends and saying, "I have no idea what to do with this issue. Do you have any ideas?" I'll do whatever I need to do to get an answer to a problem, to let someone help me see a different perspective, or to spend an hour with someone who has already walked down this road successfully. Don't get me wrong; there's still the need to fast and pray and to get the answer from God. But many times, if you will simply be honest with a close partner in ministry, God will use that person to draw something out of you that He has already put in your heart. You just haven't been able to see it on your own.

Proverbs teaches us to get wisdom regardless of the cost. Even if it costs all you have, get understanding.[5] It's that valuable. We've incorporated this mindset into the culture of our leaders and staff as well. We all realize there is so much we don't know, and we can't be afraid to admit it. If we hear of another organization doing something we are trying to do, and they have figured out a better way to do it, we try to connect with them and learn from them. And hopefully somewhere along the way we are able to share something with them that we've learned. Many of these relationships have been huge wins for us and well worth whatever we invested to make them happen.

In Louisiana, we tend to be relational. We just come into your house, grab a Coke from the fridge, and sit on your couch. We use your bathroom, borrow your lawn mower, and never even feel like we need to ask first. We just get up into your space, and we're ready for you to get up into ours. If I have it and you need it, just come get it. And if you have something I need, don't wonder where it is when you come home and it's gone.

If I have it and you need it, just come get it. And if you have something I need, don't wonder where it is when you come home and it's gone.

That's how many of our relationships with other churches work. A great example of this is our relationship with Stovall Weems and Celebration Church of Jacksonville. Stovall is the kind of guy whom I know will do anything for me, and he knows I'll do anything for him. He's probably the biggest LSU fan in Florida, so each year I have him come to Baton Rouge and speak to Healing Place Church during football season. Because of the great relationship between our churches, we have sent our Cooking for Christ team to Jacksonville several times to help them with some of their big events. When it came time for us to put together the funds for our Mobile Medical Clinic, Celebration Church was one of the first in line to help out.

When we build relationships with one another and work together as ministries and organizations, we increase each other's capacity to accomplish greater things than either of us could do alone.

Another example of the value of ministry relationships can be found at the Angola Penitentiary.[6] This prison is one of the largest penitentiaries in the United States, housing over five thousand inmates, and it is just a few minutes away from our St. Francisville campus. On our own, it would be tough to put together a massive outreach for all the inmates. Instead, we have developed a great relationship with Joyce Meyer Ministries.[7] They have a huge heart for prison inmates, and an excellent track record of ministry in prisons. We partnered to do a prisonwide evangelistic event a couple of years ago. We provided the food and a ton of workers. It was an incredible success, and we continue to build on the momentum that was started that day. Because of a great relationship, we are able to participate in a very exciting, successful, and effective outreach that is still bearing fruit.

There are hundreds of stories like this that show how God has blessed us with favor in relationships. Because we have put such a high value on building relationships over the years, our servolution has gone to a level we never could have reached by ourselves.

THE INTERSECTION OF NEED AND RELATIONSHIP

Our servolution cuts a much wider path when we connect with other like-minded churches and organizations. As your church discovers the nature of the servolution God has designed for you, you'll recognize more needs within your community and around the world than you can possibly handle. Trying to sort out where to invest your time, money, and energy to meet this immense need can be overwhelming.

You could spin a globe, close your eyes, and stick your finger down somewhere to decide where you're going to serve. However, I think it is much wiser to follow the favor God has given you and work with the relationships He has already blessed you with. Work with those you know and trust, and allow God to expand these relationship circles along the way. You'll find that you gain more and more trusted relationships, and soon you'll be connected to a lot of people who are doing what you would do if you were there yourself. This is exactly how our Mozambique campus came about.

Located near Maputo, Mozambique, in southern Africa, Nkobe is made up primarily of straw huts built in the sand, though a few homes are built with homemade concrete blocks. The only access to clean water is from wells. The residents are people who have been rejected by society, homeless and poor, living in areas too war-torn and rural for the government "welfare" system to reach them. The government, doing what it could to help, gathered them up and dropped them in Nkobe. Sounds like a great place to start a church, doesn't it?

Let me rewind about seven years. I was riding in a white mini-van on a highway in eastern Zimbabwe with Dave Ohlerking and a few other guys from our church. Hosting us was a Zimbabwean, Dave Van Rensburg,[8] who was serving at the time as the Africa Director for Children's Cup. We were learning about some of the work Children's Cup[9] was doing with AIDS orphans in Zimbabwe, and we were near Mutare, on our way to one of their sites, when Dave pointed toward a range of small mountains.

"Just over those hills is Mozambique," Dave told us in his very cool accent, sounding like an exotic tour guide. "It's where thousands and thousands of refugees fled Mozambique during the civil war during the 1980s." He went on to tell us more, but I wasn't really listening anymore. The instant Dave began speaking, God dropped something in my heart that I wasn't expecting.

I'm going to have you do something in Mozambique one day. I knew it was God, but still, I wondered. We didn't know anyone in Mozambique, and there were plenty of things we were trying to do to help Children's Cup in Zimbabwe.[10] There was more need in Zimbabwe than we had the ability to meet, and it didn't look like Children's Cup (which was relatively young at that point) would be ready to stretch to another country anytime soon.

But I couldn't shake the word from God. God had planted a seed in my heart that day on that Mutare highway and it never left me. We came home and continued to partner with Children's Cup and their work in Zimbabwe. We made sure our congregation was informed about the work that was being done in Africa. But whenever we'd put a big Zimbabwe flag out, I'd always make sure we had a Mozambique flag placed right next to it. We weren't doing anything in Mozambique, but I knew in my heart that it was coming.

Several years later, through some key relationships with people on the ground working hard to make it possible, the opportunity came for us to go into Mozambique. I visited Mozambique with Dave Ohlerking and Dave Van Rensburg, and during our time there we started the lengthy process of acquiring land in the Nkobe community. A couple of years later, we started building a church at the highest point in Nkobe. We painted it bright yellow and orange. (Yeah, it stands out like crazy.)

If it hadn't been for a healthy relationship with Children's Cup, that bright spot in Nkobe would be just another barren, sandy hill. Not only is the church in Nkobe a result of the partnership of Healing Place Church and Children's Cup, but there are others who joined us in the project. Mission of Mercy[11] and The Family Church of Lafayette[12] each paid for a large part of the construction, and the church in Nkobe now serves as a Children's Cup care point. Every day, the children in the Mission of Mercy child sponsorship program are cared for and loved through this church. Just one year after launching, the Healing Place Church campus at Nkobe had over five hundred attending every weekend.

It may have taken seven years, but God used these committed ministry relationships to powerfully fulfill what He had promised me in the shadows of that mountain range in Zimbabwe.

Placing a high value on significant relationships is one of the keys to doing anything great in the kingdom of God. Just as it is true in a healthy marriage, building powerful and intimate relationships takes time, effort, and the willingness to extend yourself to embrace others. My friend David Meyer[13] puts at the end of all his emails, "Together we are better." He's got it so right!

SERVOLUTION STRATEGY

Relationships are *everything*.

Good friends around you will inspire you to greater heights, believe in you even when you are walking through a valley, and help you carry the load of the ministry. Without great men and women around you, life and ministry get hard—and very lonely.

1. *Energizing friendships.* Who around me believes in me and in the call that God has placed on my life? Who makes me feel energized and built up on the inside after I have spent time with them? Who are the friends I know I can trust completely?

2. *Investing in others.* Am I a good friend? Do I initiate calls, texts, or emails? Do I look to encourage the friends around me? Am I fun to be around? After spending time with me, do others feel energized and built up?

3. *Authentic relationships.* Am I real with my friends? Do I feel the freedom to let it all hang out and to communicate about areas of vulnerability in my life? Do I ever share my fears or mistakes with my closest friends?

4. *Keep the door open.* Do I keep an open mind and heart to new people God may be bringing into my life?

5. *Value differences.* Am I comfortable only around people who are just like me? Do I have friends who are out of my comfort zone, who can see things in my life and ministry from a different perspective? Who are they?

PICKING UP THE TOWEL

We cannot let them get away. People are the top priority to God. As a church, as believers, we must make our top priority the same as God's top priority: the poor and hurting of our community, the people who don't yet know Jesus. If we will start at the top and get that right, then everything else in our lives will fall in line.

One of my favorite speakers is Paul Scanlon[1] from Abundant Life Church in Bradford, England. He taught something a while back that illustrated this very clearly for me. The ordering of our priorities is like getting dressed in the morning; if we try to button our shirt by starting someplace in the middle, the shirt gets all messed up and crooked and we look like we just walked off the set of *Hee Haw*. But if we start at the top and get the first button right, then the rest of the shirt acts right and ends up straight. It's the same with our ministries. If we'll just get God's top button right, the rest will be taken care of; we will never have to worry about where the money for the new building is coming from or how quickly our church attendance is growing; all the other buttons of life and ministry will fall in line and work out perfectly.

As the body of Christ, we are the ones who *have* been reached, and it is up to us never to drift away from this top priority of God: those who have not yet been reached. He chose us, pursued us, and rescued us from our dead-end lives, and once we have said yes to Him, God uses us as a resource to reach others. He loves us and proudly says, "I choose you; now I can use you." As He gazes upon us, He sees not only our lives but also the lives of the others whom He wants to love through us. He sees the millions of people who desperately need a revolution sparked in their lives, and He calls us to be the servolutionaries to ignite that fire.

My vision for this type of revolution came many years ago, on a Sunday night while I was in Bible college. I was praying at the altar at the end of a church service, expressing my dreams to God and telling Him that I was willing to do whatever He asked of me. In my heart, God showed me a picture of what He had in mind for my life. I was bent down, carrying a massive burlap sack on my back. I was straining under the weight. The sack was dirty. It was filthy. It had that been-at-the-bottom-of-the-garbage-dumpster-for-two-years kind of aroma.

Then I happened to notice the contents of the load I was carrying. The sack was filled with people. It was stuffed to the point of bursting with people who had been thrown away by life. Hurting people, wounded people, sick people, depressed people, lonely people, confused people, poor people — these were people no one else wanted. I knew that God was giving me a vision for my life.

At first, I was overwhelmed by the call, by the heaviness of the load God was asking me to bear. But as I began to walk out this vision, I came to see that I would never have to carry the burden alone. If I would lead others with humility and openly express my heart and passion for these hurting, oppressed people, God would gather and grow a large team of individuals willing to put their shoulders under the weight of that burlap sack and carry this load to the feet of Christ. This massive burlap sack — full of hurting, rejected, and precious people — symbolizes our servolution, and it has been a continual reminder of our mission as a church.

IT'S TIME FOR YOU TO PICK UP THE TOWEL

A servolution is rumbling through the body of Christ all across the world. We are a revolutionary army of people ready to take up the mandate of God's number one priority. We are unwilling to let those who do not yet know Jesus get away! We are aggressively pursuing the lost, the forgotten, and the poor so that we can show them a God who is passionately in love with them. We stand together with one heart, to do "whatever, whenever," so that the others will not get away. We are committed to serving others and showing them the hope that comes only from knowing Jesus Christ.

It's time to put down this book and to join the movement. One option is to put this book back on your shelf and think, "Wow, that sure is an inspiring story." You'll probably forget about it tomorrow. Or you can decide to act *today* and respond to God's call.

It's time for *you* to pick up your towel and join the servolution. There are no excuses worth someone else's eternal life. With God's help, you can lead a servolution that can revolutionize your city. The troops are followers of Christ, the companies of soldiers are churches, and the weapons are towels for service. Once you have experienced the sense of purpose that comes from serving others with your time, resources, and every bit of energy you possess, you'll find yourself wanting to serve more and more. And so will your entire team. Through our lives, through our families, and through our churches, God is about to touch the lives of millions of others in ways we never dreamed possible.

We can't let them get away.

SERVOLUTION TOOLKIT

The online version of this Servolution Toolkit can be found at http://www.servolution.org. What I've included in this appendix is just small part of what you'll find online, so I strongly encourage you to take a few minutes to check it out.

Okay, I hope by this point, you're ready to start a servolution in your community. In this section, I've included some ideas that can help. Some of them you'll probably have heard of before, and some were included in the chapters of the book, but I hope many of them will be new to you.

I've included some examples of how we've carried out these ideas at Healing Place Church too. The point in telling you the stories is not so you can do exactly what we did, but just to give you a clearer picture of how the outreach can work. You'll have to adapt the ideas to your own situation and community.

ESTABLISHING A PRESENCE IN YOUR COMMUNITY

It is a great thing for people to know the church is there for them. But helping them believe it means more than just spending money to advertise on billboards and in newspaper ads. Those things alone will not create the level of positive energy a servolution needs to have. There are lots of great ways to simply do small acts of kindness in our communities. Here are a few ways we've done this.

On Valentine's Day, we sometimes go to a shopping mall and hand out to senior adult women carnations that say, "Happy Valentine's Day, from Healing Place Church." We often go onto the LSU campus and hand out hundreds of packs of gum. When it is time for school to start in our community, we like to do giveaways providing children with school supplies. None of these outreaches are high-cost, but they are definitely high-value because they are high-touch. The opportunity to make a personal impact on people is much higher in these outreaches than in just running an ad in the paper.

If a billboard is the only way your community ever hears from you, they may never do anything more than know your name. But when you hand a lady a carnation with a note of encouragement from your church, then when she sees your billboard, she just might take the step to try to learn more about the people who cared enough to show her some love on Valentine's Day.

The question you have to keep asking yourself is, If we closed down tomorrow, would anybody notice?

Your honest answer to this question will determine how effectively you are establishing your presence in the community. Remember, it's not just about billboards, mail-outs, or phone directory ads. A name is just a name until you are able to make an impression of generosity and love for them to associate with that name.

We try to approach media and advertising like this: rather than just buying radio airtime for generic church ads, one year we did a short, noncheesy message each week. We figured that if we'd just be ourselves on the radio, then people would at least know our heart was to serve them and to value them. The ad directed the listener to the church at the end, but the point was really just to encourage and to give a thought of advice to the person stuck in traffic.

Another time, a serial rapist was loose in our community. For about six months, this man carried out a string of incidents in which he kidnapped, raped, and killed a woman. Needless to say, our community was dealing with a ton of grief and a whole lot of fear. We began holding prayer meetings focused on our community. But we also ran a spot on television, not about our church but simply offering encouragement and support to the people in our community. It was just another way to reach out and express our concern for people in a trying time. Remember, it's not about establishing a presence so that you can be the most popular church. It's about a sincere desire to love and to serve your community because you have something to offer that can change their lives forever: the love of Jesus Christ.

Here's a another way we've embedded ourselves into the community. But this idea is not for the faint of heart. More than once, we took a crew of volunteers and went around to dozens of local businesses and asked if we could clean their bathrooms. We went inside and said to the person in charge, "We just want to serve some of our local small businesses. Would you allow us to pick up trash on your property and clean your restrooms? It's all free."

People were usually a little shocked and said something like, "Why would you want to do that?" So we told them, "We're from Healing Place Church, and we want to show you God's love and let you know we're here for you."

It is important to let you know that we didn't just choose nice-looking, already-clean businesses to go to with this outreach. Some of the places were plain-old nasty dirty. But believe me, the impact of this kind of service went much deeper than if we had gone into these places and simply handed them a card with the time of our services on it.

Look around your community with eyes to see what needs to be done, then be the person who grabs the towel and does it.

FIFTEEN IDEAS TO HELP YOU GET STARTED

A servolution is not an event; it is a culture. Infusing this culture into the DNA of your church will change your view of the world and your perspective of the needs of those who live around you. This movement is rumbling throughout the body of Christ, a revolutionary army of people ready to take up this mandate. We are pursuing the lost, the forgotten, and the poor to show them a God who is passionately in love with them. We stand ready with one heart, saying, "I will serve others and show them the hope they can have in Jesus."

In this section you'll find several simple and inexpensive ideas that can help ignite a servolution in your church. These ideas are not just outreaches or community service projects; they are culture-catalysts for your church. So take these ideas, put them into action, and watch as God does something incredible in your community, your church, and also in you!

1. Give away bottled water. We have seen hundreds of people come to our church because one hot, Louisiana summer day they were handed an ice-cold bottle of water in Jesus' name. This may have been the first time they experienced "serving with no strings attached," and they were impacted for eternity. It's a simple, practical way to let God's love for others shine through you.

I think it's worth telling you about one family that was given some water at an intersection while they were visiting Baton Rouge. They were so inspired about the idea that they went back to their home church and did their own water giveaway. One man they gave a bottle of water to actually came to their church the following weekend and wound up giving his life to Christ. Everyone celebrated a tremendous win for the kingdom.

The sobering part of the story is that just a few days later, the man passed away unexpectedly. Thank God someone handed him that bottle of water. Thank God someone handed that family some water on their visit to Baton Rouge.

What we might think of as a random outreach is really anything but random when God is guiding it. He knows who will be there at the intersection on that afternoon. And He knows how to connect the dots.

2. Adopt an inner-city block. Organize a team from your church to go to an area in your community that is showing signs of neglect. You can pick up trash, mow the lawns, and do general cleanup. Taking responsibility for a run-down block gives the residents respect for themselves and also lets them know there are people who care for them right where they are.

3. Start a cooking team. Everyone loves to eat! Find people in your church who enjoy cooking and start a cooking team—a group that can prepare, cook, and serve meals for church and community activities. Cooking and serving a meal in the name of Jesus Christ meets a practical need and opens the door to relationships and evangelism.

4. Provide free auto maintenance. Widows, single mothers, and military wives are women who don't need the burden of vehicle maintenance. Take a day to work on their cars. It has been such a blessing to the ladies of our church and community when we offer free, basic car care (changing the oil, fixing windshield wipers, and changing out filters, for example). As a bonus, go the second mile and offer free refreshments and pampering (manicures, pedicures, and massages) to the ladies while they wait. It's a great way to just go over the top and show God's love in a practical way.

5. Serve as the cleanup crew after community events. Stay up-to-date on community events in your area and offer to serve as the cleanup crew. You probably won't be refused! You will gain favor in your community and help to make Jesus famous.

6. Serve widows. The Bible makes this one really simple: "Religion that God our Father accepts as pure and faultless is this: to look after orphans and widows in their distress."[1] Take some time to visit a widow—maybe bring her a meal or offer to take care of some odd jobs at her house. Bring her flowers and let her know she is loved and precious. One of the ways we have been able to bless widows is by doing their yard work. Watch how God blesses your church when you bless the widows in your community. It is such a basic idea, but so pure.

7. Be active on your local college campus. University campuses are full of truth-seeking people who need the love of Jesus. When classes are set to begin, have a team offer to help new students find their way and get moved into their dorm rooms. There may also be international students who could use assistance getting accustomed to the area. It's a great opportunity to connect with people who are new to your community.

8. Serve your local government. Contact your local government officials and offer to serve them any way you can. Put aside any differences you may have and show them God's impartial love. There may be ways that the church could help them accomplish goals that they've been unable to accomplish on their own.

9. Serve the homeless in your community. Regardless of why someone is homeless, homeless people still need to be reminded that God loves them, cares about them, and has a plan for their lives. One way to reach out to the homeless is to serve breakfast once a week for them right where they are. Offer to pray for them, and if they're ready, assist them in finding work and shelter.

10. Start a free food pantry. Let your church be a place where people in your community can come to receive groceries when they're struggling financially. This opens up an amazing opportunity to build a relationship with families and give them a chance to meet Jesus, the Bread of Life.

11. Give free coffee to those in the emergency-room waiting area. If you've ever been to an emergency-room waiting area, you know how slowly time seems to pass. What better time to show up with a free cup of good coffee? You can be a blessing to nurses and doctors as well. Energy drinks, good coffee, and snack bars are all generally welcomed. This outreach is simply God's people seeking out the hurting.

12. Give away school supplies. You can be a huge blessing to underprivileged families as they prepare for the new school year by picking up a school supply list and collecting backpacks and supplies such as pens, pencils, and paper. This is a great way to connect with families and show God's love in a practical way.

13. Reach out to single moms in need. Another act of kindness is assisting single moms in many different ways. You can offer to help them move, mow their lawns, run errands, or babysit. These precious ladies bear the weight of responsibility for the entire family and can always use extra support. Oftentimes, single moms don't want to ask for help, so watch for ways to serve them.

14. Respond to crisis and tragedy in your community. It doesn't matter how big or small your community is, sooner or later someone will face tragedy. It might come in the form of a house fire, a car accident, the loss of a loved one, the loss of a job, or maybe a natural disaster. The body of Christ should be first to respond to the needs of people who are hurt by tragedy. If you want to be where Jesus is, embrace those in pain.

15. Connect with other groups who are already serving your community. There are many reputable organizations that already work with cancer victims, cerebral palsy sufferers, and those with other physical handicaps. There are so many ways that you can get involved and reach out to touch those who need God's love.

Leverage your resources by finding someone who is already serving and assist them with the load they're carrying. When we come together to serve the common goal of helping people find hope in Jesus, we are much more effective than we could be on our own. And when all is said and done, showing people the love of Jesus is what it's all about.

A COUPLE MORE IDEAS FOR YOU TO TRY

Meet people on their way out of bars at closing time. At about 2:00 a.m., visit the bars in your community with bottles of water and juice to give away. It's amazing how receptive people are in this situation. Many have come to the bars looking for fulfillment and relief from the pressures of life. What better place for the church to be, offering the love of Christ at the point of need?

Give roses to ladies working at strip clubs. Women who work as strippers or prostitutes are in desperate need of knowing they are loved and precious. We have found that when we take roses, small gifts, and notes of encouragement to their dressing rooms at the clubs, there is an overwhelming response. They are stunned that a church would actually care about them and feel they are valuable.

Because of the nature of this outreach, we are very careful about who participates. We don't just let anyone go. First of all, everyone who is going to take part must be spiritually prepared. This is huge. Another key strategy is to have clear roles for the men and women on the team. While our women are inside the club, the men stay outside and connect with the club's bouncers and security staff. It is often in these outside-the-club conversations that we earn the favor that allows us the access we need to serve the ladies.

BUILD UP OTHER CHURCHES

Don't allow yourself to see other churches as competitors. We are on the same team, and ultimately we're all trying to populate heaven. It is a good idea to continually look for ways to honor other churches, to encourage them, and to help them succeed. It is not uncommon for a staff member or another church to tell me, "Hey, the people at such-and-such church need to purchase air-conditioning window units. Do you want to help out with this?" Most of the time, particularly if it is someone we are already in relationship with, we'll jump on board to help them get what they need. There are probably fifty churches in town that at one time or another we have been able to help in some way. There are also hundreds of churches around the country who have helped us somewhere along the way.

We have to initiate positive relationships with other churches in town. Just a few ideas:

- Call another pastor and invite him and his family out to dinner.
- Find out if there are items your church could donate to another church to make their services run smoother: microphones, instruments, nursery supplies, youth games, chairs, podiums, and so on.
- Invite other churches' youth groups to your youth events for free, or send some of your students to serve other churches' student ministry.
- Connect your staff and leaders with the staff and leaders in the same areas of ministry at another church.
- Invite other churches to partner with you in a community outreach.
- Invite another pastor to speak at your church.

We actually did this final item for an entire summer a few years ago. Each Wednesday night, we had a different pastor from around our community preach at Healing Place Church. The response was amazing. Trust between our churches was strengthened dramatically, and the truth that we really are on the same team became real for a whole lot of people.

Another example of church partnership is the relationship between our church and Bethany World Prayer Center. For decades Bethany has been a great church in our community, with several thousand members. The potential for competition between our two churches certainly has been there. But God has given Pastor Larry Stockstill and me a great relationship, and as a result, our churches have been able to partner in some significant ways. We worked closely together through Hurricane Katrina's aftermath. We have combined our people more than once for joint church services and concerts. Maybe the clearest picture of our relationship came when Pastor Larry and I took turns speaking in each other's churches. It was a great honor to have him speak to our people, and I was humbled to be able to speak to the incredible people of Bethany. It also cleared up all question of whether there was any competition between us.

MOBILE MEDICAL AND DENTAL UNITS

Our medical outreach is a great example of how one person in our church with an ache in her heart for a particular need can make an incredible outreach happen. Dr. Cheri LeBlanc[2] is a medical doctor in our church who came to me several years ago and told me about some medical RVs she had seen. She wanted to know if there was any possibility of our launching an outreach like this. The units were expensive and were not something we could afford, so I said, "I love the idea. Since we don't have anything like that going yet, could you start doing some medical outreaches without a mobile unit?" She got a few friends together to brainstorm.

They began going to smaller churches around our area and to one of our college campuses offering free general health examinations. They had such success with these outreaches that they developed an idea to hold a health fair for the community. We went with the idea and invited any health-care professional to participate. The day ended up becoming a huge event. Our auditorium was packed with booths offering cholesterol screening, chiropractic exams, eyesight tests, and hearing tests, just to name a few. There were even a couple of RVs outside for breast exams and prostate screenings. Everything was offered for free, and more than fifteen hundred people participated.[3] In addition, there were places to register to be organ donors, places to receive massages, and people ready to offer information about physical therapy. It was phenomenal.

Showing how much she carries the true heart of servolution, Dr. Cheri told me she wanted to do this outreach at other churches. Because we had made so many contacts that day, it was easy to invite professionals and plan these health fairs at other locations.

It was a good thing too, because just when these outreaches were really beginning to roll, Hurricane Katrina hit. Thousands of individuals had evacuated without their medications or had monthly prescriptions that had expired. Think about it: elderly people were without their medications. People who had been living on dialysis or with serious chronic conditions had little or no access to their treatments. People on medication for bipolar disorder or manic depression were without their medications for the first time in years. People had lost their prescriptions, and finding medical records for them was nearly impossible.

Needless to say, health care suddenly became a primary concern for a whole lot of people. Dr. Cheri and her team set up a makeshift clinic at the hurricane relief shelter at our Donaldsonville dream center and began visiting different shelters as well. Fifty-six churches in the area had become shelters, and she and her team did their best to serve them all.

With so many of the doctors in our area relocating to other parts of the country, we began to recognize that the need for health care of this kind was not going to go away anytime soon. We found a group based in Portland, Oregon, that provides mobile medical clinics for people all over the world. After visiting us in Baton Rouge, the team at Medical Teams International[4] told us they thought we should consider purchasing a mobile medical clinic. We felt it was right, and so we called some of our friends who have a heart for this type of outreach and asked them to partner with us to make it happen. Because of their kindness and the trust we had earned in those relationships over the years, it wasn't long until "Ele"[5] was rolling onto the Healing Place Church property.

Dr. Cheri noticed the next huge need was for a dental outreach. Many people were coming to the medical unit needing serious dental care. This RV was harder to find because there aren't many dental mobile units equipped to perform oral surgeries sitting around ready to be purchased. When Joyce Meyer,[6] one of the most generous people I know, found out we needed $115,000 to purchase this kind of unit, she wrote a check for the entire amount! Thank God for great relationships with some godly, servolution-minded ministries.

Here's what a typical Healing Hands Ministry[7] outreach looks like today: we use a parking lot at a church or a community center and we pull up with the medical and the dental units. We set up tables, sitting areas, music, and balloons for the children, and many times we cook lunch for everyone. We also always have a few trained chaplains onsite who talk with everyone who comes for an examination. They get to know the patients, ask them how their lives are going, and whether they need prayer for any needs. In 2007, we served fifteen hundred patients. Every patient was prayed for, and we saw seventy people receive Jesus. And 471 teeth were pulled; now, that's a lot of teeth!

Okay, so you may be thinking that this is a great story and you're glad it worked so well for us. But don't skip over this one too quickly. You very well may have a doctor or medical professional in your church whom God is speaking to about starting a medical outreach. Don't worry about whether you have enough money to do it; do what you can with what you have. We didn't start out with a medical RV. We just started serving people with what we had, and God took it from there.

MULTISITE CHURCH

Many churches have found that having multiple locations is a great way to extend their reach into their communities. By providing multiple options of location, style, service time, and setting, a church can appeal to a wider range of people than with just one Sunday 10:00 a.m. service at one location.

In 2004, we added our first two multisite locations, and we added seven more campuses in the next four years. I think it is important that in developing multisite strategy, churches keep in focus the language, spiritual climate, and economic condition of the community where a campus is to be located. Our strategy should be less about whether the campus can support itself financially and more about whether we are willing to commit to do whatever it takes to meet the needs of the people in that community. A big part of that question can be answered by considering the relationships you have in the area. Look for the intersection of need and relationship.

Because this has been our strategy, when you look at our campuses on the surface, no two of them are alike. One campus is in a rural area, with mostly long-time residents who love to hunt and who know pretty much everyone else in the community. Another campus is in a community in the heart of one of the poorest zip codes in our nation. We have two Spanish-speaking campuses reaching a huge growing segment of our community. Two of our campuses are on the other side of the world, smack in the middle of African communities dealing with the AIDS pandemic and abject poverty. Each of our other campuses is equally unique.

With such a diverse collection of cultures being served by our campuses, it is absurd to think that we can be effective as a church if we try to force each campus to be exactly the same as the other campuses. Some of our campus pastors wear goatees; some shave clean. Some have a little grey in their hair; some work a hairstyle with a little messy-spike action. Some of the team members tuck their shirts in, others go tails out, and others even wear a tie once in a while. (And yeah, they get funny looks when they do.) We decorate the mirrors in the bathrooms one way at one campus, another way at another campus, and maybe not at all at yet another campus. There are simple things that make each campus unique. And that's okay, because we don't reach out only to one type of community or demographic, so we do our best to ensure that a campus takes on the flavor of the community it serves.

SERVOLUTION DAY

While it is true that servolution is more than just an event, there is a huge win in setting up an event periodically to just gather everyone together and blitz the community with outreaches all over the place. Here are a few outreaches we did in one Servolution Day event recently:

- Dream Center Block Party: inflatable games, free food and drinks, three-on-three basketball tournament, face painting.
- Battered Women's Shelter Outreach: cleaning, remodeling, and renovating at the shelter, plus giving the women a very special day of pampering.
- Foster Homes Outreach: cleaning foster homes inside and out.
- Downtown Block Cleanup: picking up trash, cutting grass, and washing houses.
- Downtown School Cleanup: clearing debris, washing, painting, and doing minor repairs.
- Water Giveaways: handing out free water at busy intersections.

- Car Washes: just plain-old free car washes, no donations accepted.
- Nursing Home Outreach: visiting, playing games, reading aloud.
- Snacks to Hospital Employees: energy bars, coffee, cookies, juice.
- Outreach to Children's Wing at a Local Hospital: playing games, giving away toys, reading aloud.

Along with the games, cleanups, and giveaways, here's what really happened: we prayed for people, offered hope, fed the hungry, visited widows, played with orphans, and shared the gospel. Hundreds and hundreds of volunteers reached out and touched thousands of lives. That's how God does math!

CHRISTMAS OUTREACH

A few families in the church had an idea how they could help others, and it has become a part of how we do Christmas at Healing Place Church ever since. Here's a post I put on my blog that describes the outreach:[8]

This weekend we gave out Wal-Mart vouchers to people who needed help this Christmas. We just took a few minutes in our service to let people know that if they had a need for some help this Christmas that a gift card to Wal-Mart could help, then they should let us know after service. We had people ready to meet them, pray with them, and actually hand them gift cards to Wal-Mart based on how many people there were in their household.

Four families in our church gave to make all of it possible. I thought about Luke 14, where Jesus talks about inviting the poor and you will be blessed; although they cannot repay you, you will be repaid in heaven. That's what this was all about. We'll give away vouchers at all our campuses this weekend totalling $26,000.

And one thing I really like about it is that we have several families in the church who are ministering to the people we are giving the vouchers to. The families needing the vouchers are loved on and prayed for as they are given the vouchers. They are sent away doubly blessed.

Thank God for those who gave to make it happen, and thank God for the honor of being part of this family — a place where people can receive.

DREAM CENTERS

The ultimate goal of everything we do is to point people to Christ. A dream center is a place where people can come to find hope and learn about God's dream for their lives, and where those dreams can be fueled. We have found dream centers to be a great way to create an environment where people can find hope on the bottom shelf, where they can reach it.

We have two dream centers (Baton Rouge and Donaldsonville), modeled after the ones in Los Angeles and St. Louis. We set up our dream centers with specific targets in mind: women, children, drug addicts, and the unemployed.

Here's a typical scenario: a woman comes to the Baton Rouge Dream Center, telling us she needs help because her husband was just put in prison and she has no job. We help her with all the information she needs to apply for state aid, then assess her skills to help her find a job. All the way through the process, our goal is to help people spiritually. If they are dealing with anger, violence, resentment, or bitterness, we are ready to walk with them through this difficult season of life.

Our first dream center is in Donaldsonville, about forty-five minutes south of our Highland campus. Donaldsonville is in one of the poorest zip codes in our nation. It has some of the highest rates of incarceration and unemployment you'll find anywhere. We began serving the community and soon were ready to set up something more permanent. We decided to start a dream center which would also serve as our church campus for Donaldsonville.

After we served there a few years, city officials approached us about a school they had recently closed. It was in relatively good condition, but they just didn't need it anymore. They asked if we would be willing to take it over and use it for outreach to the city. Uhhh, yeah! The place was huge! It had tons of space for programs we had dreamed of doing but simply didn't have the room to do in our original location. Now we are able to hold church services in both locations in Donaldsonville, and we use both as dream center facilities. It is an amazing testimony of God giving us favor through our servolution in a community.

Our other dream center is in downtown Baton Rouge. There is a church that was built in 1946 on Winbourne Avenue, and it was a huge influence for the gospel in our city for many years. But through the years, their ability to influence the community diminished, and they did one of the most honorable things I have ever seen a church do. They invited another church to use their facilities to serve the community. Because of some relationship connections, they knew about our heart to serve the people of Baton Rouge, and they chose us.

The facilities are tremendous. There is a two-story building with a huge room that serves as a cafeteria and a meeting room. Then there's the big brick and stained-glass sanctuary. They have allowed us not only to use the classroom building but also to hold church services in the sanctuary. What a blessing!

We have known for a while that one of the biggest unmet needs in Baton Rouge is shelter for mothers with children. One of the greatest advantages of this facility is that the upstairs has several rooms that have been set up as a shelter for those needing temporary lodging. Putting two and two together, we decided that this could be the perfect opportunity for us to take on the need for shelter for mothers with children.

One of the coolest things about a dream center is that it provides the opportunity to serve in dozens of ways. Here are a few ways we're currently serving from our Baton Rouge dream center:

Saturday outreach. Every Saturday we meet at the Baton Rouge Dream Center for a downtown outreach. Our goal is to find ways to serve the community, whether it's going door to door with groceries, visiting widows, doing yard work, or picking up trash. Every week, dozens of volunteers give up their morning to reach out to the lost, to remind people of their value, and to make a difference in somebody's life. We serve people, pray for them, and watch God make a way where there appeared to be no way. Through simple acts of kindness, we have seen salvations, healings, and hope restored. Not a bad way to start your weekend, right?

Prisoner reentry initiative. One of the outreaches that we've begun is a prisoner reentry program that helps recently released offenders to develop life skills and to find meaningful employment. Along with job training and education, we also provide case management and mentoring to nonviolent, non-sex-related offenders. We also are able to guide them through the process of enrolling in government assistance programs that many people in this situation never benefit from simply because they don't know how to access the help. There are lots of people in our community who are in need of a second chance. Our volunteers are able to be a part of offering new hope and restoration.

After school program. Every week we open our doors to the youth in the community. In an effort to build relationships and offer positive avenues of recreation, we offer young people ages twelve to eighteen the chance to be involved in sports, crafts, dance, art, cooking, tutoring, computer classes, and other educational opportunities. We teach classes on abstinence and goal setting, allowing kids the opportunity to have a safe place to ask the tough questions.

Many of the young people in north Baton Rouge face huge challenges at home. These challenges include single-parent and blended families, poverty, absent fathers, and continual violence. Drug addiction is rampant and youth are often forced to make destructive choices just to survive. Unless something changes, it is likely that more young men from this area will go to prison than to college. We want to be the "something" that happens to change this.

Street youth outreach. It is hard to think about the reality that there are homeless youth and child prostitutes in our community. Unfortunately, just because we are uncomfortable with the idea doesn't mean it isn't reality. Within forty-eight hours of running away from home, most young people will be contacted by a pimp, a drug dealer, or both.

Our goal is to reach kids before we lose them to the street. In an effort to bring hope into some of these seemingly hopeless situations, we began an outreach to homeless youth. We hit the streets offering food, hygiene kits, and a listening ear. Our goal is to develop enough trust with these young people that they will allow us to help them to seek another path in life.

Along with our street outreaches, we also offer a drop-in center where homeless and at-risk youth can take a shower, wash their clothes, and spend some time with people who really care. When we're in the streets, we provide contact information to our twenty-four-hour hotline for youth and families who are seeking help. We partner with several other organizations that provide shelter services, should these kids choose to get off the streets.

Homeless outreach. Once a week we head out early to serve a hot meal to homeless men and women in downtown Baton Rouge. So often these precious people are overlooked and ignored by society. By simply providing a free meal and a listening ear, we can make a huge difference in their lives. Many of the people we meet at this street breakfast get plugged into Friday Thrive, giving them an opportunity to hear God's Word and find fellowship and purpose for their lives.

Midnight outreach. Once a month we go to the streets in search of those who have somehow lost their way and have found themselves involved in drugs, violence, and the sex industry. Whether they're dancing at a strip club or selling drugs on a street corner, we believe that God still has a purpose for them. Through handing a dancer a rose or giving a drug dealer a cold bottle of Powerade, we have seen simple acts of kindness speak volumes about the love of God. The majority of those we meet on these outreaches do not go to church, so we take the church to them. Through consistently showing up where they are, we have developed relationships with people who are typically hard to reach.

We received a letter one time from the mother of one young lady who received a rose during one of these outreaches. She told us her daughter had been stunned by the kindness shown to her by people from a church, and it had made her rethink how she felt about God. This precious mom said her daughter was quitting her job and returning home to Alabama. Thank God for the power of a simple act of kindness done with great love!

Small Group Teaching and Discussion. We do all we can to help men and women develop the tools necessary to live the lives God intends for them and to give them a sense of purpose. Through teachings, group discussions, fellowship, and service opportunities, God is restoring a sense of purpose and significance in the men and women of this community.

We work with the homeless, drug dealers, prostitutes, single parents, and those struggling just to make it through the day.

Hosting short-term missions teams. From street outreach to medical clinics, everything we do is made possible by volunteers. We are blessed to be able to host teams from across the nation who come to serve at our dream centers, enabling us to take the church to the streets. Teams are housed on-site and have the opportunity to participate in outreaches, service projects, and one-on-one ministry. They not only learn about what we do; they get to experience it for themselves, up close and personal. Through hosting short-term missions, we can empower others to take what they learn here and adapt it to their cities. We want to see a servolution ignited all over the world, and this is one way we have found we can spread the movement.

Clothing boutique. It's actually a simple idea, but it is so effective in giving dignity to people in need: a free-clothing boutique giving people the opportunity to "shop" for new or nearly new clothes. Many of the outfits we provide show up on our pews for Sunday service. We get to provide people not only with clothing but also with a sense of dignity.

And this clothing boutique isn't just a free version of a thrift store; we have some tight guidelines regarding what donations we accept:

1. We accept new clothes or clothes that look like they're new. We want clothes that are fashionable and stylish (from this decade; not your high-school band uniform).
2. We accept new socks and underwear. (We accept nothing in this category that has been worn.)
3. We accept new or nearly new towels (no holes, stains, or ragged edges).
4. We accept new or nearly new shoes, like flip-flops, tennis shoes, and hiking boots.
5. We accept couches, chairs, mattresses, and beds that are new or nearly new.

The point is that we don't want to offer people trash. If you call it junk, then don't bring it and offer it to someone as a treasure.

We want to build people's sense of value and let them know that they are precious to God and to us. We want to give people our best, just like God gave us His best. Our heart is to offer people hope, dignity, and the Word of God, and sometimes it all starts with some new clothes.

SERVOLUTION RESOURCES

The purpose of this section is to give you a quick look at some of the key partnerships we have made in our servolution that may prove valuable to you as you launch your own servolution.

GREAT ORGANIZATIONS TO HELP YOUR SERVOLUTION

Children's Cup (www.childrenscup.org). Children's Cup's purpose is to take humanitarian and spiritual aid into the hard places where war, natural disasters, and epidemics have devastated societies. Through a network of dozens of "care points," Children's Cup offers medical, educational, emotional, and spiritual support to the children of the community.

Children's Cup is the organization we have partnered with to establish our Africa campuses. The Christ-centered humanitarian work they do so faithfully has opened some tremendous doors for the gospel in southern Africa.

Cyrus International (www.cyrusinternational.org). Cyrus International is a nonprofit charity committed to confronting the atrocities of human trafficking, neglected orphans, and domestic substance-abuse victims. Cyrus specializes in providing accountability, transparency, and serving as a resource base for organizations around the world that are making an impact for oppressed people. Through strategic partnerships, Cyrus provides hope and helps to restore the lives of these victims. Cyrus also collects and distributes finances, resources, and business skills to humanitarian organizations on the forefront of this fight. By uniting as an army demanding social justice, we believe we can make a difference.

Cyrus is headed by Lee and Laura Domingue, who have become incredible friends and partners for DeLynn and me in the global mandate of reaching others. Their integrity, compassion, and wisdom are great assets for the kingdom. Because of that, they are becoming the hub of interaction for many of the missionaries we are connected with. Lee's book, *Pearls of the King*, is more and more being recognized as a spiritual textbook on the potential in relationships between pastors and key business leaders in the church. Check out the book at http://www.pearlsoftheking.com.

Equip (www.iequip.org). Operating from their belief that every person is born with the potential to influence others, Equip is training a global vanguard of men and women who are stepping forward to effectively confront the greatest needs on our planet. With the Great Commission as their priority, these devoted leaders follow the leadership-development model demonstrated by Jesus, who spent the greatest amount of His time in public ministry training a group of leaders to impact the world.

Equip was founded by the amazing John Maxwell, who has been a great friend to Healing Place Church for several years now. Our involvement with Equip's Million Leader Mandate in Italy has opened up several doors for us. Training leaders and pastors in Italy initiated and developed several relationships that continue to be anchors for an Italian servolution.

Equip and Empower (www.equipandempower.com). Equip and Empower wants to see every person on planet earth reached with the gospel, individuals fulfilling their God-given destiny, and the local church flourishing. Their A21 campaign stands for abolishing injustice in the twenty-first century by rescuing girls from sex slavery and assisting them in reentering society.

Nick and Chris Caine are part of the team at Hillsong in Sydney, Australia. Chris is one our favorite people to welcome to Healing Place Church because of the life-giving, challenging messages she consistently brings. Nick and Chris are also highly valued friends for DeLynn and me.

Joyce Meyer Ministries (www.joycemeyer.org). The heart of Joyce Meyer Ministries (particularly their Hand of Hope outreach) is to help hurting people. Each year, they serve millions of meals to the impoverished worldwide, support dozens of orphanages that rescue young boys and girls dying on the streets of impoverished nations, nurture HIV/AIDS orphans in third-world countries, help the homeless off the streets, provide clean, safe water for entire villages, treat thousands through medical missions outreaches, minister to the elderly, help troubled young women, reach out to thousands of inner-city children, and offer hope to forgotten prisoners.

Our partnership with Joyce Meyer Ministries has produced many monumental leaps forward in our outreach capacity. JMM provided so much help for us during the Katrina relief effort and has continued to be a great partner in our dream centers and mobile medical and dental units domestically as well as internationally.

Mercy Ministries (www.mercyministries.org). Mercy Ministries provides hope and healing to desperate young women who are seeking freedom from life-controlling problems such as drug and alcohol addictions, depression, eating disorders, unplanned pregnancy, physical and sexual abuse, and self-harm.

There is a huge need for ministry like what Nancy Alcorn and Mercy Ministries provide. It would be nice if there wasn't. But there is. Supporting Mercy Ministries can be one of the most effective uses of resources a church can implement.

Mission of Mercy (www.missionofmercy.org). Mission of Mercy is a child-sponsorship organization helping to meet the physical and spiritual needs of children in poverty-stricken areas of the world. Through Mission of Mercy programs, children receive food, education, medical aid, and hope in Jesus Christ.

Mission of Mercy was one of the key partners that joined with us to build the Terry Melancon Chapel, where our Mozambique campus holds church services. They are also a key part of our missions strategy through the child sponsorships they coordinate.

Operation Blessing (www.operationblessing.org). Operation Blessing helps at-risk children, teaches life skills, runs orphan-care programs, provides disaster relief, hunger relief, water wells, and medical services throughout the world.

Operation Blessing is the organization that provides much of the goods we are able to distribute through our dream centers in the Baton Rouge area.

Samaritan's Purse (www.samaritanspurse.org). Samaritan's Purse aids the world's poor, sick, and suffering, reaching hurting people in countries around the world with food, medicine, and other assistance in the name of Jesus Christ. This earns them an opportunity to share the gospel, the good news of eternal life through Jesus Christ. SP's emergency-relief programs provide desperately needed assistance to victims of natural disaster, war, disease, and famine. By offering food, water, and temporary shelter, they meet critical needs and give people a chance to rebuild their lives. SP's community-development and vocational programs in impoverished villages and neighborhoods help people break the cycle of poverty, giving them hope for a better tomorrow, and let them know they are not forgotten.

Samaritan's Purse is a phenomenal organization with a tremendous amount of integrity. Franklin Graham's vision to touch the poor and hurting in the world has produced a great team with a high standard of excellence. Their partnership is a great asset for any serious servolution.

MORE GREAT SERVOLUTIONARY ORGANIZATIONS

Association of Related Churches (http://www.arcchurches .com). ARC is all about planting life-giving churches that grow and reproduce life-giving churches themselves.

Blood:Water Mission (http://www.bloodwatermission .com). Blood:Water Mission, committed to clean blood and clean water to fight the HIV/AIDS pandemic, builds clean wells in Africa, supports medical facilities caring for the sick, and works to make a lasting impact in the fight against poverty, injustice, and oppression in Africa by linking needs with people and resources.

Book of Hope (http://www.bookofhope.net). Book of Hope's goal is to affect people's destinies by providing God's eternal Word to all the children and youth of the world.

Camino De Vida (http://www.caminodevida.com/08_ index_en.php). Camino De Vida is a large, nondenominational church pastored by Robert Barriger that reaches the poor and hurting in Peru.

Camp Barnabas (http://www.campbarnabas.org). Camp Barnabas exists to provide awesome, life-changing opportunities to people who have various forms of disability or disease. People with developmental challenges, post-traumatic burns, blood disorders, cancer, very poor vision or blindness, physical challenges, complete or partial loss of hearing, and many other diseases and challenges benefit from the inclusive environment of Camp Barnabas.

Campus Crusade for Christ (http://www.campuscrusade .com). Campus Crusade's heart is to help build spiritual movements everywhere so everyone knows someone who truly follows Jesus Christ.

Children's Hope Chest (http://www.hopechest.org). Children's Hope Chest believes that every orphan has the right to know God, experience the blessing of family, and have the opportunity to develop independent-living skills.

Coca-Cola (http://www.coca-cola.com). Everyone knows the Coke brand, but what you may not know is that they are typically very generous in local communities.

Convoy of Hope (http://www.convoyofhope.org). Convoy of Hope mobilizes, resources, and trains churches and other groups to conduct community outreaches, respond to disasters, and direct other compassionate initiatives in the United States and around the world. COH outreaches distribute free groceries, organize job and health fairs, and provide activities for children.

Exodus International (http://www.exodus-international .org). Exodus International is a nonprofit, interdenominational Christian organization promoting the message of freedom from homosexuality through the power of Jesus Christ.

Family Research Council (http://www.frc.org). Family Resource Council's mission is to defend issues regarding faith, family, and freedom in the sphere of government.

Global Expeditors (http://www.globalexpeditors.net). Global Expeditors is a mission-discipleship organization committed to empowering young people to bring the gospel to the world.

Go Global (http://www.goglobalmissions.com). The heart of Go Global is to ignite a passion for world missions and to support local churches, existing organizations, and projects through strategic partnership.

Habitat for Humanity (http://www.habitat.org). Habitat for Humanity builds decent, safe, affordable, long-term housing for families who have been affected or displaced by conflicts or disasters. They are also engaged in providing housing finance for the poor, and provide information and training on construction methods, building materials, and energy efficiency.

Healing Hands International Ministries (http://www.hhim .us). Healing Hands International Ministries is building hospitals in Honduras and gathering medical equipment, as well as training disciples.

Healing Place Network (http://www.healingplacechurch .org/network). HPC Network is a community of churches and ministries throughout the world partnering to build the kingdom. A unique aspect of the HPC Network is the high level of access to network leadership that partners are given. The network carries the DNA of Healing Place Church to be a healing place for a hurting world.

Healing Place School of Ministry (http://hpsm.healing placechurch.org). Healing Place School of Ministry equips people to carry out the will of God through the local church. Interns learn what Jesus-style leadership is all about while forming a strong biblical foundation. They also explore their life's calling while acquiring ministry skills.

Hillsong Network (http://www2.hillsong.com/network/). The Hillsong Network is a network of churches and ministries from various parts of the body of Christ that desire to connect with Hillsong Church for impartation and relationship. The Hillsong Network exists to champion the cause of the local church — *your* church.

Insight for Inmates (http://www.insightforinmates.org). Insight for Inmates encourages members of the body of Christ who are in prison, evangelizes the inmates of America, equips the saints of God who are behind prison bars, and exalts the Savior in the middle of Satan's den.

Italy for Christ (http://www.italyforchrist.it/english/index .html). Italy for Christ works to present the gospel to every Italian during this generation through and in collaboration with the local churches.

Joel Osteen Ministries (http://www.joelosteen.com). Joel Osteen is the pastor of Lakewood Church in Houston, Texas, whose vision is to make a positive impact upon the city of Houston by creating a citywide family center in which all are welcome.

Leadership Ministries (http://www.leadershipministries .com.au). Led by Brian and Bobbie Houston, pastors of Hillsong Church in Sydney, Australia. Leadership Ministries' singular, all-consuming passion is to build God's church and kingdom on the earth and see everyday people released into their purpose and calling.

Leadership Network (http://www.leadnet.org). Leadership Network fosters church innovation and growth through strategies, programs, tools, and resources that are consistent with their far-reaching mission: to identify, connect, and help high-capacity Christian leaders multiply their impact.

Los Angeles Dream Center (http://www.dreamcenter.org). Reaching the homeless, drug addicts, and prostitutes on the streets of Los Angeles. They also have now opened a dream center in New York City. Check it out: http://www.dreamcenter .org/NewYork.

Medical Teams International (http://www.medicalteams

.org). The mission of Medical Teams International is to demonstrate the love of Christ to people affected by disaster, conflict, and poverty around the world.

Mission: Water for Life (http://www.lifetoday.org/site/PageServer?pagename=out_waterForLife). Part of James Robison's ministry, Mission: Water for Life provides water wells for impoverished people. They have surpassed twelve hundred new water wells in more than twenty-five nations.

Missione Possibile (http://www.missionepossibile.com/index.php?lang=2). Missione Possibile is a missions organization based in Italy that gives first aid and concrete help to people in difficulty, through practical support like delivery and distribution of medicines, food, and clothing, financing, and developing local projects around the world.

Outreach Magazine (http://www.outreachmagazine.com). One of the greatest resources available for any church wanting to engage in a servolution is Outreach magazine. It is full of useful insights, reviews, testimonies, and a ton of ideas. Some of the greatest creative thinkers in church outreach today are contributors.

Relay for Life (http://www.relayforlife.org). Relay for Life offers everyone in a community an opportunity to participate in the fight against cancer. Teams of people camp out at a local high school, park, or fairground and take turns walking or running around a track or path. Each team is asked to have a representative on the track at all times during the event. Relays are overnight events, up to twenty-four hours in length.

Road to Jerusalem (http://www.roadtojerusalem.org). Road to Jerusalem's mission is bringing peace and reconciliation to Jews and Gentiles in the Messiah.

Salvation Army (http://www.salvationarmy.org). The Salvation Army's mission is to preach the gospel of Jesus Christ and to meet human needs in His name without discrimination.

Service International (http://www.serviceinternational.org). Service International helps people in spiritual, physical, and situational crises. While SI also provides immediate disaster relief, its focus is on complete, long-term recovery.

Shaohannah's Hope (http://www.shaohannahshope.org). Shaohannah's Hope is dedicated to helping prospective adoptive parents overcome the financial barriers associated with adoption. They accomplish this by awarding financial grants to qualified families already in the process of adopting.

Society of St. Vincent de Paul (http://www.svdpbr.com). St. Vincent de Paul strives to understand and fulfill the needs of the poor within Baton Rouge and the surrounding community. They provide hot meals to those who go hungry, warm beds to those who have no place to sleep, medications to those who cannot afford them on their own, and uniforms that children need to attend school.

St. Louis Dream Center (http://www.stldreamcenter.org). The St. Louis Dream Center's aim is to present the gospel to the lost, feed the hungry, clothe the poor, minister to the elderly, widows, and orphans, visit prisoners, reach out to people of all ages and in all walks of life, and teach people how to apply biblical truth in every facet of their lives.

Steve Sjogren (http://www.stevesjogren.com). Steve and his writings have had a tremendous impact on us, particularly early on. We continually refer to things we learned in his book *Conspiracy of Kindness* as keys to how we do what we do today.

Teen Challenge International (http://www.teenchallenge .org). Teen Challenge International is one of the oldest, largest, and most successful programs of its kind in the world. More than just a faith-based residential recovery program, TCI is a place where hope is reborn, purpose is restored, and families are made whole.

Teen Mania Ministries (http://www.teenmania.com). Teen Mania's goal is to provoke a young generation to passionately pursue Jesus Christ and to take His life-giving message to the ends of the earth.

Upward Unlimited (http://www.upward.com). Upward is an evangelistic sports ministry specifically designed for boys and girls in kindergarten through sixth grade that promotes salvation, character, and self-esteem in every child.

Venture Expeditions (http://www.ventureexpeditions.com). Venture Expeditions uses intense physical challenges, like biking across countries or climbing mountains, to raise awareness and funds that benefit hurting and hopeless people around the world.

Watoto (http://www.watoto.com). Watoto's mission is rescuing children in Uganda and raising them as leaders by placing them in the Watoto Children's Village.

Willow Creek Association (http://www.willowcreek.com). WCA works to link like-minded, action-oriented churches with each other and with strategic vision, training, and resources.

NOTES

CHAPTER : INTRODUCTION

1. Luke 19:10.

CHAPTER 1: THE BEGINNING OF A SERVOLUTION

1. Just thought it'd be cool to point out that December 16 is the day DeLynn and I got married a couple of centuries later. Not sure there's any significant application there, but I think it's cool.
2. We actually thought it would be totally amazing if somehow God would allow us to see a church grow to three hundred people. Little did we know how much bigger God's dream was.
3. Lakewood Church (http://www.lakewood.cc) was started by John Osteen and is now pastored by his son, Joel. It is one of the largest churches in the USA and is doing great things for the kingdom as a result of the seeds Pastor John planted in the church, as well as in his son's life. John Osteen is certainly one of my all-time heroes. We were in Houston visiting April and Gary Simons (John Osteen's daughter and son-in-law). Gary and April now pastor High-Point Church (http://www.highpointchurch.com) in Arlington, Texas, and continue to be some of our best friends.
4. If you were wondering whether I was going to list the scandals here, the answer is no. I don't believe details like that help anyone.
5. Our ministry to widows has grown to over three hundred widows that we visit and care for every week.
6. Acts 20:35.
7. Check out Kevin and Tracy's blog at http://mawaelife.wordpress.com.
8. We still have dinners periodically after services, but more often than that, we have coffee and donuts and bagels before services and we do larger events on the property during which we serve food — still always free — for thousands of people. The three men who cooked that first dinner went on to launch our ministry still known today as Cooking for Christ, which cooks thousands of meals every year all over the region, as well as right here at home at Healing Place Church. Cooking for Christ is an integral part of our outreach strategy.

CHAPTER 2: STRATEGIC SERVOLUTION

1. The world's best ice cream *has* to be Blue Bell Homemade Vanilla.
2. Remember these? http://en.wikipedia.org/wiki/Flowbee.
3. Mark Stermer is now one of our staff pastors and helps coordinate strategy and development of our campuses.
4. Nathan Keller now pastors Sugar Land Family Church (http://www.slfconline .com) just south of Houston, Texas, and is still a great friend and partner in ministry (even though he's in Texas). Geaux Tigers!

CHAPTER 3: THE CULTURE OF SERVING

1. Dan Ohlerking (check out his blog at http://www.danohlerking.com).
2. Yeah, that's right, the dude with the pickup truck we used for our rat bait giveaway.
3. Ken is one of our pastors who is gifted in the type of ministry that was needed in New York. He serves as a chaplain for several civil service departments (fire, police, sheriffs) in our area and is amazing in ministry to families during times of grief and loss or during hospital stays. And he does a mean Johnny Cash impersonation.
4. Remember that first church dinner I told you about? That was where it all started for Cooking for Christ. By the time 9/11 came around, the team was well-formed and ready to serve on a much larger scale than they were that first day.
5. Loosely translated from the original Cajun, that means "Oh yeah, baby! That's some good stuff!"
6. For those who either just really don't remember or who are too young to have been even a little concerned, here's a short description of the Y2K scare. When we went from the year 1999 to 2000, there were a lot of people worried that computer systems would fail to flip to the new year successfully. This is because prior to 2000, many computer programs simply used the last two digits of the year, so it was feared that going from 99 to 00 would cause calculations to assume we went 99 years back rather than one year ahead. As a result, banks could fail, and the economy could spiral down into a panic-induced depression. We understood that in case things did actually get crazy, we should be ready to serve people.
7. Children's Cup (http://www.childrenscup.org).
8. My son Dylan actually gave his life to Christ during one of the presentations of *Heaven's Gates and Hell's Flames* that we did that year. Thank you, Jesus! To learn more about *Heaven's Gates and Hell's Flames*, visit Reality Outreach Ministries' website: http://www.realityoutreachministries.org.

CHAPTER 4: SERVOLUTION IS ALL ABOUT JESUS

1. Wayne Austin is one of the people I respect the most on this planet. He is not just an amazing father-in-law; he serves on our staff as a spiritual father, a presbyter, and the leader in our counseling ministry and is just one tremendous blessing to Healing Place Church.
2. Two of my favorite verses on this are Matthew 6:33 and Psalm 37:4. If we'll seek His kingdom and righteousness, and if we'll delight ourselves in Him, He promises to take care of the rest and to give us the desires of our heart.
3. Matthew 28:19.
4. Philippians 2:7 NLT.
5. Proverbs 11:25 says, "A generous man will prosper; he who refreshes others will himself be refreshed."
6. We currently have experienced a string of four officers being killed in the line of duty in four years. Each of these deaths is a massive tragedy. As a community, we are hardly accustomed to dealing with these rare, but not rare enough, situations.
7. Terry's mother wrote Terry's story in a book titled *End of Watch*. I recommend it highly. You can find it here: http://www.endofwatch.org.

CHAPTER 5: HURRICANE KATRINA

1. Steve Robinson is a great friend who pastors Church of the King (http://www.churchofthekinginfo.com) in Mandeville, Louisiana, right in the bullseye of Hurricane Katrina.
2. The concept of "it is amazing what can be accomplished if no one cares who gets the credit" was taught by John Wooden, the legendary coach of the UCLA basketball team during their unmatched stretch of ten NCAA championships.
3. Pastor Larry Stockstill is the pastor of one of our country's great churches, Bethany World Prayer Center, just a few miles from Healing Place Church here in Baton Rouge (www.bethany.com).
4. Pastor Jacob Aranza is the pastor of Our Savior's Church (www.oursaviorschurch.com) in Broussard, Louisiana. He's like a big brother to me.
5. Our Annex campus is about a mile away from our main offices at the Highland campus.
6. I had started blogging at http://www.dinorizzo.com just a few months prior to Hurricane Katrina, and during the post-Katrina relief effort, the blog proved to be a valuable tool for us in our communication with those around the nation who were seeking ways to help.
7. Matthew 25:40.

CHAPTER 6: SERVOLUTION TOP TEN

1. John 13:34.
2. Mark 12:33.
3. Isaiah 61:1.
4. Louisiana's own world-famous hot sauce (http://www.tabasco.com).
5. You *gotta* have some Tony Chachere's Cajun Seasoning if you're gonna call it fried catfish (http://www.tonychacheres.com).
6. John 10:10.
7. 3 John 2 NKJV, emphasis added.

CHAPTER 7: THE FABRIC OF A SERVOLUTION

1. Check out Donna Frank's blog: http://donnafrank.blogspot.com.

CHAPTER 8: UNLOCKING THE NEED

1. Oswald J. Smith, the great Canadian pastor, evangelist, and missionary statesman during the 1800s.
2. That's right, the controversial group led by Louis Farrakhan.
3. Find out more about Kibera at http://en.wikipedia.org/wiki/Kibera.
4. Luke 10:30 – 37.

CHAPTER 10: THE COST OF A SERVOLUTION

1. Craig Groeschel pastors LifeChurch.tv, a totally amazing church. Check out his blog: http://swerve.lifechurch.tv. He was also kind enough to write the foreword for this book. Thanks, Craig.

CHAPTER 11: NO EXCUSES

1. In case you're wondering, it was the Milwaukee Braves over the New York Yankees in seven games. Just didn't wanna leave you hanging on that one.
2. Pamper nights are definitely not a thing for the menfolk at Healing Place Church. We invite the women of Healing Place Church to bring ladies who are friends and family to a night during which they are just simply pampered. It's over the top, with manicures, petit fours, free gifts, great music, and a ton of other stuff just to make them feel valuable.

CHAPTER 12: SERVOLUTION STREET

1. Very popular in Cajun cooking, andouille (pronounced ahn'-doo-wee) is a coarse, spiced, smoked pork sausage with pepper, onions, and seasonings.
2. Those tiny rings you get when you chop the top of a green onion.
3. Natalie Spera. Check out her blog: http://www.nataliespera.com.
4. Healing Place School of Ministry: http://www.healingplacechurch.org/hpsm.
5. Go Global: http://www.goglobalmissions.com.

CHAPTER 13: KEEP YOUR SERVE ALIVE

1. Matthew 18:23–35.
2. Yardbird: poultry (most commonly chicken), generally cooked either on a grill or battered and deep-fried with plenty of spice and presented in generous quantities for consumption by humans.

CHAPTER 14: NEVER SERVE ALONE

1. Matthew 4:18–22.
2. James 5:16.
3. Hebrews 3:13.
4. Galatians 6:2.
5. Proverbs 4:7.
6. According to Wikipedia (http://en.wikipedia.org/wiki/Louisiana_State_Penitentiary), Angola was once known as "the bloodiest prison in America," but it has made a tremendous turnaround, much of which has been attributed to the influence of faith-based programming.
7. Joyce Meyer Ministries is one of the greatest partners we have had through the years. Their heart for the world is huge, and their commitment to make a difference through partnerships is strong. Check them out: http://www.joycemeyer.org.
8. Dave Van Rensburg later went on to work for Joyce Meyer Ministries in Africa and continues to be a great friend to Healing Place Church and Children's Cup.
9. Children's Cup (http://www.childrenscup.org) is an international relief organization. In chapter 3, I mentioned that we were honored to partner with them in our response to 9/11. However, Children's Cup focuses much of its work in Africa. Through their network of care points, thousands of orphans and

vulnerable children are cared for daily. Many of these children are battling the effects of the AIDS pandemic, abject poverty, and lack of basic education.

10. Children's Cup was founded in 1992, and in the last several years, it has grown tremendously. It now serves children all over the southern part of Africa, including care points in Zimbabwe, Swaziland, and Mozambique.

11. Mission of Mercy is one of the great ministries that we enjoy calling our friends. They work with child sponsorships for kids all over the world and have a tremendous level of integrity. We can testify to this from working with them on both sides of the equation — hundreds of people in our church sponsor children through Mission of Mercy, and we've seen their integrity in that process. And we've seen how they work it out on the ground with the children through their partnership with Children's Cup. Check out Mission of Mercy at www.mofm.org.

12. The Family Church of Lafayette (www.thefamilychurch.cc) is pastored by a friend of mine from my days in Bible college, Jay Miller (http://www.pastor jaymiller.com). Jay has been a faithful friend over the years and is seeing God do amazing things through their church about forty-five minutes west of us in Lafayette, Louisiana.

13. David is World Missions Director for Joyce Meyer Ministries. Of all the cool things I could say about him, I think at the top of this list is that he's a great friend.

CONCLUSION

1. Paul Scanlon is the senior pastor of Abundant Life Church, a great church with a great story to tell of God's faithfulness to them. Check out their website: http://alm.org.uk.

APPENDIX 1

1. James 1:27.

2. Check out Dr. Cheri's blog: http://drcheri.blogspot.com.

3. This includes three hundred volunteers from the church, another three hundred medical professional volunteers, and about nine hundred people who came to receive services.

4. At the time, Mobile Teams International was called Northwest Medical. Check them out at http://www.medicalteams.org.

5. "Ele" is our medical team's nickname for the mobile medical unit. The name is short for *eleos*, the Greek word for "merciful" as used in Matthew 9:13. It is kindness or good will toward the miserable and the afflicted, joined with the desire to help them.

6. Joyce Meyer Ministries helped us acquire a mobile dental clinic a couple of years ago.

7. For more information about Healing Hands, check out http://store.healing placechurch.org/ministries/outreach/?page_id=13.

8. My blog: http://www.dinorizzo.com.

About the Leadership Network Innovation Series

Since 1984, Leadership Network has fostered church in-novation and growth by diligently pursuing its far-reaching mission statement: *To identify high-capacity Christian leaders, to connect them with other leaders, and to help them multiply their impact.*

While specific techniques may vary as the church faces new opportunities and challenges, Leadership Network consistently focuses on bringing together entrepreneurial leaders who are pursuing similar ministry initiatives. The resulting peer-to-peer interaction, dialogue, and collabo-ration — often across denominational lines — helps these leaders better refine their individual strategies and accel-erate their own innovations.

To further enhance this process, Leadership Network develops and distributes highly targeted ministry tools and resources, including books, DVDs and videotapes, special reports, e-publications, and free downloads.

Launched in 2006, the Leadership Network Innovation Series presents case studies and insights from leading practitioners and pioneering churches that are success-fully navigating the ever-changing streams of spiritual renewal in modern society. Each book offers *real* stories, about *real* leaders, in *real* churches, doing *real* ministry. Readers gain honest and thorough analyses, transferable principles, and clear guidance on how to put proven ideas to work in their individual settings.

With the assistance of Leadership Network — and the Leadership Network Innovation Series — today's Christian leaders are energized, equipped, inspired, and enabled to multiply their own dynamic kingdom-building initiatives. And the pace of innovative ministry is growing as never before.

For additional information on the mission or activities of Leadership Network, please contact:

LEADERSHIP ❈ NETWORK®
800-765-5323
www.leadnet.org
client.care@leadnet.org

Leadership from the Inside Out

Examining the Inner Life of a Healthy Church Leader

Kevin Harney

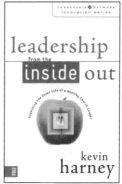

You can serve God and his people for a lifetime and do it with passion and joy. You do not have to become one of the growing number of leaders who have compromised their integrity, character, and ministry because they failed to lead an examined and accountable life.

The road forward is clearly marked. Leaders must decide to humbly and consistently examine their inner lives and identify areas of needed change and growth. Also, wise leaders commit to listen to the voices of those who will love them enough to speak the truth and point out problems and potential pitfalls.

Kevin Harney writes, "The vision of this book is to assist leaders as they discover the health, wisdom, and joy of living an examined life. It is also to give practical tools for self-examination." Sharing stories and wisdom from his years in ministry, Harney shows you how to maintain the most powerful tool in your leadership toolbox: you. Your heart, so you can love well. Your mind, so you can continue to learn and grow. Your ears, your eyes, your mouth... Consider this your essential guide to conducting a complete interior health exam, so you can spot and fix any problems, preserve the things that matter most, and grow as a source of vision, strength, and hope to others.

Softcover: 978-0-310-25943-5

Pick up a copy at your favorite bookstore!

Sticky Church

Larry Osborne

In *Sticky Church*, author and pastor Larry Osborne makes the case that closing the back door of your church is even more important than opening the front door wider. He offers a time-tested strategy for doing so: sermon-based small groups that dig deeper into the weekend message and velcro members to the ministry. It's a strategy that enabled Osborne's congregation to grow from a handful of people to one of the larger churches in the nation—without any marketing or special programming.

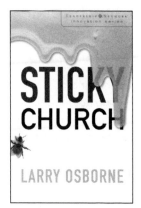

Sticky Church tells the inspiring story of North Coast Church's phenomenal growth and offers practical tips for launching your own sermon-based small group ministry. Topics include:

- Why stickiness is so important
- Why most of our discipleship models don't work very well
- Why small groups always make a church more honest and transparent
- What makes groups grow deeper and stickier over time

Sticky Church is an ideal book for church leaders who want to start or retool their small group ministry—and velcro their congregation to the Bible and each other.

Softcover: 978-0-310-28508-3

Pick up a copy at your favorite bookstore!

Deliberate Simplicity

How the Church Does More by Doing Less

David Browning

Less is more. And more is better. This is the new equation for church development, a new equation with eternal results.

Rejecting the "bigger is better" model of the complex, corporate megachurch, church innovator Dave Browning embraced Deliberate Simplicity. The result was Christ the King Community Church, International (CTK), an expanding multisite community church that Outreach magazine named among America's Fastest Growing Churches and America's Most Innovative Churches. Members of the CTK network in a number of cities, countries, and continents are empowered for maximum impact by Browning's "less is more" approach. In *Deliberate Simplicity*, Browning discusses the six elements of this streamlined model:

- Minimality: Keep it simple
- Intentionality: Keep it missional
- Reality: Keep it real
- Multility: Keep it cellular
- Velocity: Keep it moving
- Scalability: Keep it expanding

As part of the Leadership Network Innovation Series, *Deliberate Simplicity* is a guide for church leaders seeking new strategies for more effective ministry.

Softcover: 978-0-310-28567-0

Pick up a copy at your favorite bookstore!

The Monkey and the Fish

Liquid Leadership for a Third-Culture Church

Dave Gibbons

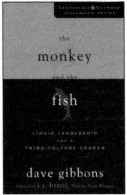

We need fresh, creative counterintuitive ways of doing ministry and leading the church in the twenty-first century. We need to adapt. Fast. Both in our practices and our thinking.

The aim of this book is simple: When we understand the powerful forces at work in the world today, we'll learn how something called third culture can yield perhaps the most critical missing ingredient in the church—adaptability—and help the church remain on the best side of history.

A third-culture church and a third-culture leader look at our new global village and the church's role in that village in a revolutionary way. Third culture is a way to reconnect with the historical roots of what Jesus envisioned the church could be—a people known for a brand of love, unity, goodness, and extravagant spirit that defies all conventions.

Softcover: 978-0-310-27602-9

Pick up a copy at your favorite bookstore!